Heke TANGATA

Heke TANGATA
Māori in Markets and Cities

Brian Easton
for Te Whānau o Waipareira

Oratia

Published for Te Whānau o Waipareira Trust by Oratia Books,
Oratia Media Ltd, 783 West Coast Road, Oratia, Auckland 0604,
New Zealand (www.oratia.co.nz)

Copyright © 2018 Te Whānau o Waipareira Trust
Text copyright © 2018 Brian Easton

The copyright holders assert their moral rights in the work.

This book is copyright. Except for the purposes of fair reviewing, no part of this publication may be reproduced or transmitted in any form or by any means, whether electronic, digital or mechanical, including photocopying, recording, any digital or computerised format, or any information storage and retrieval system, including by any means via the Internet, without permission in writing from the publisher. Infringers of copyright render themselves liable to prosecution.

ISBN 978-0-947506-43-8

Front cover: Photograph of protesters on the Maori Land March, College Hill, Auckland. Ref: PA7-15-17. Photograph by Christian Heinegg; Alexander Turnbull Library, Wellington, New Zealand.
Back cover: Dame Whina Cooper and her granddaughter Irenee Cooper setting off for the Land March, 14 November 1975. Photograph by Michael Tubberty; New Zealand Herald Archives Neg: 1557c (215). Courtesy newspix.co.nz

Printed in China

CONTENTS

Foreword by *John Tamihere*   7

Introduction   9

Part One

1. Rural Beginnings   15
2. Urban Migration   23
3. The End of the Golden We(a)ther   32
4. The Shift to More-Market   38
5. Retrenching the Welfare State   45
6. The Māori Corporates   50
7. Māori Community Responses   57
8. Māori Today   63

Part Two

9. Being Māori   71
10. Demography   75
11. Educational Attainment   82
12. Employment   91
13. Health   98

14. Incomes	104
15. The Criminal Justice System	112
16. Wealth and Housing	119
Endnotes	123
Index	129

FOREWORD

The narrative around matters Māori is often framed in socio–historical terms. Te Whānau o Waipareira determined that this never-ending Māori story would benefit from having the voices of individuals and whānau telling their experiences. This would ensure their actual struggles, trials and tribulations were set down, documenting the dynamic cultural evolution that has seen the rise of Māoritanga within a pan-tribal, urban context.

These stories are told in the book entitled *Urban Maori: The Second Great Migration*. The socio-historical story has therefore been captured at this moment in time.

No society evolves solely within this construct, however. There are political and economic drivers that help shape the historical narrative, which is what the present book explores.

We approached Brian Easton to author this work because he is a nationally recognised economist. Just as importantly, he is unbridled in crafting a non-partisan economic work that lets the facts and figures speak for themselves.

Māori, as with all indigenous populations around the world, are disproportionately represented and seemingly locked in at the bottom of every socioeconomic indicator. Brian's work, first documented in the report 'Maori Meets the Market' and now published as *Heke Tangata*, goes a long way in explaining the economic context of Māori post the Second World War.

As a consequence, it is a teina to its tuakana *Urban Māori*, and completes the present story of honouring those that sacrificed and suffered in order to evolve and construct Māori communities and marae in the cities.

John Tamihere
Chief Executive Officer, Te Whānau o Waipareira
Tāmaki-makaurau, February 2018

INTRODUCTION

Tēnā koutou katoa.

I was delighted to be invited by Te Whānau o Waipareira Trust in 2016 to report on the experiences of post-war Māori. Over the years I had worked on the topic as a social statistician characterising the state of Māori, as an economist working for iwi on Māori claims, as an historian integrating the Māori story into the total narrative, and as a policy analyst working on a variety of governmental issues. Here was a chance to synthesise all that previous work, update it, and explore issues that I had only touched upon previously.

This book publishes the report I prepared for the Trust. Its whakapapa goes back to that marvellous collection of essays *The Maori People Today: a general survey*, edited by Professor Ivor Sutherland and dominated by Sir Āpirana Ngata, which described the state of Māori some 80 years ago. Much has changed since. Māori were then primarily rural; today most live in big cities. It is not merely their location that has changed, although that change by itself has been large enough, disrupting traditional whānau connections. Today's Māori engage with the economy in quite different ways from how their ancestors did only a few generations ago. That has been all the more challenging because the economy has been changing. While overall there has been much progress and higher material standards of living, many of the changes have been inimical to Māori, and public responses have not always been helpful.

Part One of this book is a narrative of post-war Māori experience. Chapter 1 describes the situation 80 years back, explaining how rural communities were not sustainable because of demographic and economic change. Chapter 2 describes the second great Māori migration, into the cities. Under any circumstances this movement would have been difficult, especially when public policy was not supportive, but the difficulties were compounded by the catastrophic fall in the price of wool in 1966 described in chapter 3. For over a century the crossbred sheep industry had been at the centre of the New Zealand economy; almost overnight its profitability collapsed and for two and more decades, at the time of the main urbanisation of Māori, the New Zealand economy struggled to cope. Inevitably the new arrivals in the cities would be most affected. As chapters 4 and 5 describe, the policy responses of opening the economy up to markets and rolling back the system of government support for those in need were particularly damaging to Māori. Meanwhile, they had to adapt their rural-based culture for a new urban-based situation. Chapter 6 describes the evolution of the tribal-based institution, iwi; chapter 7 outlines how new — typically non-tribal — institutions evolved in response to urban demands, The final chapter of Part One summarises these discussions.

Part Two is a statistical inventory of the state of Māori covering definitions (chapter 9), demography (10), educational attainment (11), employment (12), health (13), incomes (14), the criminal justice system (15) and wealth, including housing (16). The inventory confirms the narrative of Part One: Māori may have successfully navigated the second great migration, but they are a generation behind the Pākehā population.

Te Whānau o Waipareira gave me no direction on what I should write, although they asked that I pay attention, greater than is common, to Māori who are the Trust's clients and are often poorer and less attached to their iwi than most. Where judgements are made they are mine; no one else involved in the project need agree with them. Any errors are mine too.

My general approach has been not just to catalogue what has happened but also to provide a framework for thinking about what may happen, even if this involves challenging the conventional wisdom (which always lags behind the fact). That is why, for instance, chapter 9 has had to pay more attention to how to define Māori, given the fluid evolution of the notion. (In any case a social statistician has to be sensitive to definitions.) What will happen to Māori and Māoridom will become evident only in the future, but my hope is that this work will be seen then as having provided a foundation for tracing, and perhaps even influencing, those changes.

I am grateful to a number of people for assisting in writing this book. First, I pay tribute to Ngata, Sutherland, Horace Belshaw and the other contributors to *The Maori People Today*. I would hope that this study is seen as a successor, although I could not hope to be as influential. Second, I would like to thank John Tamihere and his team at Waipareira Trust, not only for commissioning this study but also for helpfully assisting me whenever I asked. Similarly, albeit at a later stage, Peter Dowling, Carolyn Lagahetau and their team at Oratia Books have converted my manuscript into a handsome publication. Many officials and academics, too numerous to mention here, have helped with various issues when they have come up; I have thanked them personally. Finally I would like to thank gratefully and gracefully for her support, Elizabeth Caffin, who has helped in numerous ways; without her this would have been an inferior product.

I have considerable faith in the future of Māoridom even though it will be different from the present. Looking at the sweep of Māori history, since their ancestors first arrived in Aotearoa about 700 years ago, and certainly since the arrival of the European 200-plus years ago, one is struck how, despite great stresses and shocks, Māori and Māoridom have flourished. This has happened by adapting to new circumstances while maintaining core values. The process has not always been understood by some, who see Māori as if there has been little change and that Māoridom is to be judged as it was, not as it is becoming.

As the Duke in Giuseppe Tomasi di Lampedusa's novel, *The Leopard*, said to his nephew, 'If we want things to stay as they are, things will have to change.' In translation, this could be the whakataukī for Māori development: 'Ki te hiahia he ao toitū ngā tikanga o tēnei wā — me mātua whakarere ka aua tikanga.'[1]

Ngā mihi,
Brian Easton
Wellington/Te Whanganui-a-Tara
September 2017

PART ONE

CHAPTER 1 — RURAL BEGINNINGS

It is widely, but wrongly, believed that after the New Zealand Wars of the 1860s, Māori were demoralised from their defeats and had become a dying race. That cannot be true since not all Māori were defeated — some fought on the Crown side, while others were not involved. Even the defeated often adapted with dignity, as Keith Sinclair records in *Kinds of Peace* (1991). The dying myth arises from the declining population in the late nineteenth century, reaching a nadir in about 1896. But, as Ian Pool (1991) shows, the recovery in Māori fertility occurred much earlier, even though the effects of past events on mortality among adults disguised the recovery.

While much Māori land was confiscated, not all was seized and some was returned. (Boast and Hill 2009) The land that Māori cultivated tended to have two disadvantages. First, it was often badly connected to the rest of the economy; improving transport connections was not a priority of the non-Māori central government. Second, much Māori-owned land was unsuitable for sheep farming, which was the leading economic sector. About 60% of Māori lived north of Lake Taupō where the land — affected by the Taupō volcanic eruption of circa 233 CE — suffered either from mineral deficiencies that caused bush sickness or was swamp that caused footrot. In fact, south of Taupō, Māori sheep flocks were roughly the size of those of non-Māori but Māori numbers were proportionally fewer than the rest of the population. By the time dairying (unaffected by footrot) became really significant after 1900, especially in the Waikato, Māori were generally so impoverished that, unlike Pākehā, they lacked the capital to take advantage of the new leading sector. (Easton, forthcoming)

Instead, for the first part of the twentieth century the Māori economy was primarily subsistence based. By 'subsistence' it is meant that communities were largely self-sufficient, although there would have been some activities for the purpose of generating cash for needs that the local economy could not supply. As Sir Āpirana Ngata wrote:

> There are Maori communities which are satisfied to live on minimal reserves, where they grow the vegetables they require, from which they make seasonal excursions into the labour field to obtain the minimum resource for the purchase of clothes and food, and where they rusticate [live a country life] between periods of employment. (Ngata 1940: 152)

Such a life had not been unique to Māori: many settlers living on small farms in the middle of the nineteenth century had led a subsistence-like life, supplemented by cash received from wages from roads boards and the like. But meat and dairy exports had revolutionised their farming, enabling the transition from subsistence to the commercial farming that is today's norm.

Māori were not as successful. Their land was not as close to freezing works, dairy factories and ports; it was generally less fertile and less developed. Under reigning land laws, titles to Māori land holdings were complicated, divided among many owners and sometimes disputed, so lenders were unwilling to advance capital for development. Māori developers had little leverage of their own. As long as they were subsistence farmers, it was difficult to accumulate the capital or the reputation required by lenders to break out of the low-development trap.

The Structure of the Māori Economy, 1901–51

The Census reports the number of Māori almost trebled from 45,549 in 1901 to 134,862 in 1951. However, what constitutes 'Māori' depends on definitions. The 1901 figure covers those who were classified as 'solely Māori' (i.e. from 'half-caste' to full blooded). The 1951 figure represents those of Māori descent. In 1951 115,676 reported they were 'solely Māori', an increase of 2.5 times. The total population was 2.4 times larger. However, it seems likely that, given widespread intermarriage, Māori gene numbers grew less than 2.4 times.

There is only limited data on the early-twentieth-century Māori economic structure.[2] The 1901 census asked about livestock. Māori reported ownership of 1.6% of the total sheep, 3.0% of the cattle and 23.0% of the pigs. At the time they comprised 4.8% of the population. Even allowing for under-reporting, with the allowance that Māori were a more rural people, the conclusion remains they were not greatly into livestock farming.

Occupations were first asked of Māori in 1926. The figures for the 1926 and 1951 census are summarised in Table 1.1.

Table 1.1: Census-reported Occupations of Males and Females (Percentage)

	1926		1951	
OCCUPATION	MĀORI	NON-MĀORI	MĀORI	NON-MĀORI
Primary production	74.9	27.3	36.2	18.8
Industrial	13.4	25.8	36.6	33.6
Transport & communications	3.9	11.3	8.7	10.7
Commerce & finance	0.8	16.1	2.9	17.2
Services	6.9	19.7	15.6	19.8
TOTAL NUMBER OF WORKERS	14,440	561,848	32,625	71,0371
Females as a % of total	19.6	21.8	20.6	23.3

Source: 1926 and 1951 Censuses (occupational classifications may differ)
Notes: In 1926, 'non-Māori' includes a few urban Māori.

The discrepancy between the occupations of Māori and non-Māori in 1926 is so large it needs little detailed comment, but a review of the subcategories is instructive.

Almost half of Māori described themselves as working in the farm sector (probably including those involved in shearing). While there were some fishermen, trappers, miners and quarrymen, the only other significant primary activity was forest occupations. (Many in the farm sector would have fished and hunted, and those in other occupations — or their spouses — were often involved in supplementary farm activities including gardening.)

The next largest occupation after farming was labouring: about a quarter of the total. The size of the industrial group may seem surprising, but the largest subcategories are (in order): factory hand, roadman, sawmiller, well-sinker, carpenter and freezing worker. There were 279 adult men classified as clerical or professional, of which 104 were clergymen and related occupations; the next largest group were 46 interpreters.

The 1951 Census shows some convergence of the occupations between Māori and non-Māori, but Māori were still far more in the farming sector. They had caught up in manufacturing, construction and infrastructural activities, but remained behind elsewhere. The closest were services — clergy were less prominent — but at a finer level, Māori fell into the categories that are less skilled. More than half of Māori in manufacturing were in food processing, including at freezing works, and about a quarter were in sawmilling and the simpler wood processing, so the vast majority were in some kind of rural manufacturing.

Some lived in towns or small urban areas. The Statistics New Zealand definition of 'urban' is a town of 5000 people or more. (For these statistical purposes, a Māori who shifted from the town of Kaitaia to the city of Auckland has not changed their urban status.) In 1926, some 15% of Māori met this definition of urban living; by 2006, it was more than 84%.

Revealingly, in 1926, apart from Auckland and Wellington, the largest urban centres of Māori were Gisborne, Napier and Whanganui, which also had substantial Māori settlements around them. Numbers in these urban areas — with the exception of 1162 in Auckland (the total Māori population was 69,780) — were about the size of a large hapū. More than 70% of Māori were located in the Auckland region, from North Cape to East Cape. So in 1926, Māori workers were a rural people; even those who lived in the small urban centres were barely separated from their rural roots.

During the quarter century after 1926, Māori began moving away from direct land-based industries because their land could not employ them all. Despite more land being brought into production, only 4000 of the extra 24,000 jobs in 1951 were in primary production. The new farming methods were land intensive, so jobs per acre were diminishing, and those relying on the subsistence economy were being displaced.

There was some movement to the cities in the interwar period. Perhaps the Great Depression delayed the drift in the 1930s; it is sometimes argued the rural–urban drift accelerated during World

War II. However, it was a trickle compared to the urbanisation flood after the war.

The Māori People Today

As the interwar period came to an end, the Institute of Pacific Relations published *The Maori People Today*, which summarised the views of a number of informed people about Māori in 1940. Edited by Professor of Psychology Ivor Sutherland, the eight luminaries contributed 12 chapters. Three were by Sir Āpirana Ngata, who also shared a fourth with Sutherland; Ngata seems to have had considerable involvement in all the remaining chapters.

By today's standards it is a strange collection; there is little attention to Te Tiriti o Waitangi or the New Zealand Wars. While there are a number of references to population trends, there is no chapter on them (which indicates the importance of the pioneering work from the 1960s of Ian Pool, and those who followed him). The lack of a sustained demographic analysis meant the logic of Māori population growth overwhelming rural employment was not properly realised.

Presumably the book contained the most progressive thinking of its time. If so, it is instructive that, with one exception, the issue of urbanisation that would dominate post-1940 Māori life was not really on the agenda. The exception is the chapter on economic circumstances by Professor of Economics Horace Belshaw. He set out the problem as follows:

> Estimates based on observations, on discussions with Maori leaders, and on information from Departmental sources, would suggest that when existing freehold land is fully developed about 5000 farms will be established, supporting say 20,000 people or one-quarter of the present population. This will leave 60,000 [three out of four] not provided for by farming on native lands even if the population does not increase. (1940: 190)

Belshaw concluded, '[E]ven though the above estimates may be subject to a wide margin of error, there is an unambiguous picture of a people whose land resources are inadequate, so that a great and increasing majority must find other means of livelihood.'

While there was considerable variation by region, he concluded that '[n]o tribe has sufficient land to support all its people'. (1940: 190)

He, and indeed the rest of the writers, underestimated the subsequent population growth. Suppose the rate of natural increase was 2% per annum from the nadir of 42,113 in 1896. In 2006 the Māori population would have been about 370,000, or about three-fifths of the actual level, and there would be correspondingly fewer Māori in farming had the occupational structure remained unchanged. But even under this scenario, there would have been a shortage of land.

Belshaw went on, after considering the various characteristics of Māori workers (reported below):

> It will be suggested later that the Maori will be required to seek work away from his community. Loyalty to the community and love of locality add to the social costs of movement. He may migrate for a time, but his roots are in his tribal territory and the pull of his community is strong. Tribal loyalty, in addition to being a source of strength, is also a factor impeding the mobility of labour. These are not the only impediments to his movement. The Maori migrant to Auckland or Wellington is still an alien in a foreign city, a city which makes no response to his inner needs. To economic risks must be added the hazards of social maladjustment, which may be difficult to overcome because tribal differences among the migrants make it difficult to establish a genuine Maori Community of interest. Often he is ignorant of the opportunities for work which are available, and his prospects are darkened by the colour of his skin; not because of racial prejudice in its cruder forms, but through doubts of his capacities and sense of responsibility. (1940: 195)

He expected Māori would find employment in other rural activities (including public works). Had Belshaw had projections of likely employment trends — like those available 15 years later — he would have been very gloomy about Māori rural prospects.

The prospects were further undermined by Māori educational attainment; Belshaw devotes almost of a fifth of his chapter to it. There is also an entire chapter by Douglas Ball, a former Senior Inspector of Native Schools, who concludes, 'The problem with adult education is concerned with the great body of Maoris living in rural communities, whose education and standards of living could not, by any stretch of imagination, be called adequate. From these people has come no cry for further education.' (1940: 305)

There are two critical points here. First, Māori formal education was judged inferior to that received by non-Māori, and by someone with intimate knowledge of it. Second, adult education may have been necessary but there was little demand for it. The lack of demand probably reflects that Māori educational achievement was judged by them to be perfectly adequate for their subsistence mode of life. It would prove inadequate for urban Māori.

Belshaw's conclusion that Māori would find it difficult to urbanise was also based on his assessment of Māori character. He devotes two pages to this, from which it is hard to extract anything without giving the impression of racist views — although Belshaw could not have been a close colleague of Ngata if he was racist. His account may be taken as an indication of the views of a thoughtful and sensitive Pākehā of the time; it may appear biased here because the extracts focus on the limitations of Māori and do not mention their strengths, which Belshaw greatly admired and acknowledged elsewhere.

> His main limitations appear to be he dislikes working alone, and is less capable of prolonged and continuous effort. So he is liable to tire of a job and seek a change. He is slower than the *pakeha* to mature, in terms of the requirements of a *pakeha* society, and the view is widely held that he is less competent in the exercise of individual responsibility. This may only mean he is less responsible in European work and environment requiring a sustained effort. ... In general the Maori is not interested in commerce and is less efficient in the professions or callings requiring abstract thinking. His main limitations, however, arise from a lack of training, so the undoubted capacities in many directions are insufficiently developed. Even in the realms of abstract thought it is by no means certain that his limitations are other than environmental. (1940: 193)

Belshaw goes on to develop the thought that '[t]he problem is to effect a compromise between traditional attitudes and the imperatives of changing capitalism' [or urban market living]. He was not far out of line with Ngata, who greatly desired that Māori would retain their traditional culture. Perhaps both underestimated Māori adaptability or the way in which culture evolves.

We may forgive Belshaw for not quite reaching the obvious conclusion of impending urban migration of a people who were not ready for it. He carried the ball a long way up the field. He simply needed a final push to get it across the line.

Conclusion

Mass Māori migration into the cities in the post-war era was neither expected nor prepared for, even if it seems inevitable with hindsight. Moreover, even with decades of hindsight, the implications have not been fully teased out. In particular, Māori were not going to adjust to urban living and employment easily.

Bibliography

Ball, D.G. (1940), 'Maori Education', in Sutherland, I.L.G. (ed.) (1940), *The Maori People Today: A General Survey*. NZIIA, Wellington.

Belshaw, H. (1940), 'Maori Economic Circumstances', in Sutherland, op. cit.

Boast, R. & R.S. Hill (eds) (2009), *Raupatu: The Confiscation of Maori Land*. VUP, Wellington.

Easton, B.H. (forthcoming), *Not in Narrow Seas: A Political Economy of New Zealand History*. MUP, Auckland.

New Zealand Census of Population and Dwellings, 1981, *Series C Report 9. Before 1951*. Statistics NA, Wellington.

Ngata, A.T. (1940), 'Maori Land Settlement', in Sutherland, op. cit.

Pool, D.I. (1991), *Te Iwi Maori*. AUP Auckland.

Sinclair, K. (1991), *Kinds of Peace: Maori People After the Wars, 1870–85*. AUP Auckland.

Sutherland, I.L.G. (ed.) (1940), *The Maori People Today: A General Survey*. NZIIA, Wellington.

CHAPTER 2

URBAN MIGRATION

The Second Great Migration

For more than a century after the European arrival, Māori remained a rural people. Some lived in towns or small urban areas, but typically they were part of the iwi rohe (region) and their marae — with its central role in communal life — and the whānau pā (strictly a kāinga, an unfortified village) was not far away. Numbers in these urban areas were about the size of a large hapū on the 1926 Census night. More than 70% of Māori were located in the Auckland region — from North Cape to East Cape — and the city was the economic focus, a node without the ring of substantial secondary centres that was to develop in the post-war era.

There had been a steady movement to the cities in the interwar period. It is sometimes argued it accelerated during World War II; perhaps one can see this in the data, perhaps not. Perhaps the Great Depression delayed the drift in the 1930s. Regardless, it was a trickle compared to the urbanisation flood after the war. In 1951, 71% of Māori were living rurally; that majority changed in the early 1960s, and by 2006 only 16% of the total Māori population were rural.[3]

The growth was primarily in the four main centres (initially, and mainly, Auckland). They housed only one in ten of the Māori population in 1926. By 1971 four out of ten lived there, while more than two out of ten were living in other urban centres with populations of greater than 25,000. The current urban proportion — 64% in 2006 — is not overly different from the non-Māori proportion of 71% (which had crossed the 50% threshold before 1926).

Population Growth

The proportions obscure the massive population growth that was occurring. The definitions may not be comparable but the 1926 Census records 69,780 people of Māori descent; the 2006 Census says there were 643,977. However, the latter figure excludes more than 130,000 Māori living permanently overseas (and those temporarily there on Census night). Given there would have been fewer in proportion in 1926, it is not implausible to suggest that the Māori population in the world increased by a factor of 11 in 80 years — a population growth rate in excess of 3% per annum.

This is a rate somewhat higher than the maximum that demographers would normally think of as sustainable, but Māori were breaking no biological rule. Instead there was a high rate of miscegenation (inter-racial breeding).

For much of the interwar period, Māori had a high rate of fertility, in the range of six or seven births per woman. Non-Māori had been at that level in the 1880s, but over the following century they had gone through a slow transition down to approximately two births per woman by around the 1980s.

The Māori fertility rate remained high until the early 1960s, then collapsed over the following two decades until it was close to the non-Māori rate. The reasons for this exceptionally fast transition are complex, but urbanisation was most certainly one: this is evident in the differential fertility rates by location. While later urban births substantially contributed to urban numbers, much of the early stage of urbanisation was driven by migration of those born in the countryside.

The Drivers of Māori Urbanisation

What caused the urbanisation? Undoubtedly there were Māori who went to the cities because there were lifestyle, income and career prospects that a rural society was unable to provide. But while there were some very successful Tiki Whitingita (Dick Whittingtons), many more were driven into urban areas because there were insufficient prospects of economic, education and economic opportunities.

One study found migration from a region in the early 1960s was associated with poor-quality housing (probably a proxy for poorer living conditions in general), and low incomes. It could not evaluate the impact of jobs, which were also a major urban attraction.

In 1926 almost half of the Māori labour force (49.5%, or about 20,800 in total) said their main occupations were fishing, farming, forestry or mining. According to the 2006 Census, there were 16,200 Māori employed in these industries, only 7.8% of the Māori labour force.

The rural story was set out in the previous chapter. Because there were limits on the land available and because higher production was associated with lower levels of labour per unit of land (with similar limitations facing how other resources could be utilised), the primary sector could not generate sufficient employment for the growing population. In 1926 40.6% of the Māori labour force registered a farming occupation. Had the same proportion applied in 2006, there would have been about 84,300 Māori in farming. In fact, the actual total in that occupation — Māori and non-Māori — was 119,100 in 2006; under the assumption of no change in the Māori occupational structure, 70% of the farm workforce would have been Māori.

Of course there were additional opportunities in farm processing and rural servicing, but they could not contribute enough jobs either. Despite the opportunities in, say, rural freezing works, many Māori had to find work in the cities.

Moreover, in the first two post-war decades (to 1966), cities were struggling to find the labour they needed. This resulted in an economic pull from the cities coupled with the push from the countryside.

The Pattern of Urbanisation

The urbanisation was all a bit haphazard. There was no grand plan, no leader — no urban Ngata — to guide the migration. Nor were the flows even across the country; initially there was movement to local towns and then on to Auckland. This urbanisation involved much longer periods of migration and moving to the rohe of different iwi.

This is well illustrated in a study by Joan Metge, who looked at the connections between a village in the Far North (Muriwhenua) and Auckland. With a five- to six-hour drive between them, the physical connection was a far greater challenge in the early 1950s. Yet these rural and urban communities managed to stay in touch far more intimately than those involved in the thirteenth-century Polynesian migration or the nineteenth-century British migrations.

The ongoing connections were a major reason why a strategy of assimilation — expecting Māori to become Pākehā — could never work. As long as the urban dwellers were strongly attached to a rural community deeply immersed in, and fiercely committed to, its own culture, the migrants would not abandon it.

Yet Māori had to have their own institutions in their urban environment. The iwi of the village Metge studied was descended from the Kurahaupō canoe; the iwi of the Auckland isthmus was from the Tainui one. The rural migrants were manuhiri (visitors) with restricted rights compared to the tangata whenua (people of the land): rights that were integral to Māori cultural practices. If the marae was the centre of social life back home, how were the manuhiri to have a comparable centre in the territory of another iwi? Solutions were slowly found, initially thanks to the national marae in urban centres; nowadays, non-local marae of various statuses are common (the mihi that begin meetings acknowledge the position of the tangata whenua).

The notion of a chain of migrants is well understood; a few intrepid souls settle successfully in the new land, and others follow, relying on their guidance and hospitality to settle in. Māori teenagers and those in their early twenties dominated, with the women at a younger age. Later on, they seem to have taken some of their retired elders.

There is 'island hopping', in which the success of one new settlement encourages others to move on to the next city. Thus it was with Auckland. The success there was followed by migration to other urban centres. The great drive that generated the Auckland influx ended in the 1970s and population growth came from births, while other centres absorbed dispersing Māori.

The outcome is nicely illustrated by Christchurch, whose region's tangata whenua — always small — had been decimated by Ngati Toa raids in 1831. Despite being New Zealand's third-largest urban area, it had the seventh-largest Māori population in 1926 and ranked eighth in 1951. By 2006 it was fourth behind Auckland, the Wellington urban area and Hamilton.

Adapting to Urban Life

There is a sense that many migrating Māori did not adapt well to urban life, to Belshaw's 'imperatives of changing capitalism'. Because of the central economic concerns of this study, we focus here on the labour-market skills, but there were adaptation problems on the social side too (as illustrated by the problem of urban marae).

It would be misleading to say that rural Māori were unskilled.

Even those in subsistence farming had skills that today's townie can admire. A man might have to be able to fish and manage a boat, hunt and manage a gun, cultivate (although this was often women's work) and manage a modicum of livestock, and carry out numerous handymans' jobs around the house and farm. He would have to be physically strong, adaptable and able to learn from practical experience.

None of these skills were usually obtained at school, but were passed down through generations or learned on the job. Education aimed to give skills for another sort of occupational life. It is true that Ngata, Ball and Belshaw, among others, had emphasised the fundamental importance of education to Māori for their future progress, while at the same time lamenting the less-than-adequate level of Māori schooling. A later chapter reports that Māori markedly lagged behind non-Māori in educational achievement by roughly a generation — that is, this generation of Maori has (roughly) the same educational achievement as Pākehā a generation older. But in terms of Māori stuck in the sticks, the schooling system was not particularly relevant.

But post-war Māori were not stuck in the sticks; they were settling in the cities. Not many of their rural skills were relevant to urban occupations, except at the very lowest levels on the skills ladder, while their level of education limited them from ascending that ladder. (Although we shall use the term 'low skilled', in some ways it is more helpful to think of these being generic or general skills in contrast to the specific skills required for those jobs higher on the ladder.)

There has long been a central weakness in New Zealand's labour force around upskilling, because traditionally it has tended to follow the British approach to education rather than a Continental European approach. The former focuses on tertiary professional education, including a secondary education preparing students for such courses. The latter places greater emphasis on post-secondary educational and training institutions for all with strong linkages to work experience, and a correspondingly broader approach in secondary education. A nationwide system of polytechnics in New Zealand was not introduced until the 1970s, and in the 1990s government policy deliberately undercut the apprenticeship system.[4]

Instead, many skills were and are supplied by international migrants, almost as a matter of government policy. Examples go back to the 1950s, but the situation is illustrated by the planning of the rebuild following the Canterbury earthquakes. It was evident there would be a shortage of skilled workers, but from the beginning this was met by importing foreign skilled workers rather than upgrading the skills of available New Zealanders. Not only is this the default position, but it is quite likely there was a view that the existing local training arrangements did not have the capacity to meet the challenge. Five years later, there are still proposals to import labour for the next building boom.

This mindset did not have an impact solely on Māori, but because there were proportionally more Māori at the bottom of the skills ladder, they were more heavily affected. The intergenerational transfer of work skills was less effective for them, given the rural origins of their whānau.

There were, of course, jobs at the bottom of the skills ladder that rural Māori admirably filled. Typically they were manual and required no specific skills except for adaptability and willingness to work. But numbers of such jobs were not growing as quickly as jobs further up the ladder (which required specific skills, typically following formal and on-the-job training). The caveat is necessary because there is hardly any systematic data.

The falling share of low-skilled jobs was probably a slow process, rather than an abrupt and rapid one. It slowly became evident in an incipient rise in unemployment shortly after the wool-price crash of December 1966. (It disappeared from view in the early 1970s, but became more pronounced in the later 1970s.)

Three points are relevant here. First, unemployment has a disproportionate impact on low-skilled workers because employers will hang on to their more skilled workers, if necessary giving them the lower-skilled work and displacing those with fewer skills.

Second, the government absorbed some of the more skilled workers directly by expanding its workforce, especially in some state-owned enterprises, above a level that was commercially prudent. (Industrial development and protection favoured employing low-skilled workers.)

Third, there was probably a bias towards the elimination of low-skilled jobs (although arguably the current phase of technological change is eliminating some much higher on the skills ladder). This is nicely illustrated by the slogan 'Girls can do anything'. They were once limited by physical strength, but mechanisation has largely eliminated that handicap.

Further details of these issues and trends are given in the following chapter, illustrated by the labour-market deterioration when the supportive policies were reversed. A final caveat is that an unemployed worker is not going to get much on-the-job informal training, again setting back Māori occupational aspirations.

A Note on Māori Women in the Labour Force

This section has largely focused on Māori men. This is because their story is better understood — it is simpler and better tracked statistically. The complication for women is that in the early part of the post-war era, the majority only operated in the paid labour force until they were married or, later, until they had their first child. It wasn't until the 1970s that it became common for mothers to return to the paid labour force while their children were at school; mass early childhood education is an even later development.

Additionally, Māori and non-Māori women have tended to have their children at different ages. (The different numbers of children narrowed following urbanisation and need not detain us.) This has meant the participation ratios by age have been different. Māori women were more likely to have their children at a younger age, while their non-Māori equivalents were obtaining vocational qualifications. By having their children later, more non-Māori had established careers, whereas most Māori women were returning to the paid labour force after childcare without vocational qualifications and with less experience. Their path to low-skilled work was perhaps different from that of Māori men, but the outcome was much the same.

An issue debated in the 1970s was whether ßpaid working mothers displaced unskilled males, and so were a cause of their unemployment. I investigated this but could find little evidence; the two groups were not competing for the same jobs.

The Pākehā Migration Comparison

The urbanisation described here for Māori also occurred for Pākehā, but a couple of generations earlier. During the middle of the nineteenth century, they too were largely a subsistence-based rural society — yet they adapted much more easily to urban life. Why?

First, they went through much of the transition to the commercial (that is, Belshaw's 'capitalist') mode of economic operation while they were still on farms; many Māori went directly from subsistence rural living to urban living.

Second, Pākehā received better formal education; their informal (adult) education was also more extensive.

Third, they arrived in the urban centres first and adapted them to Pākehā ways. By the time Māori arrived Pākehā had been there for two generations; Māori were a minority who had to fit in with the dominant Pākehā framework.

Fourth, because of their earlier migration — largely from Britain — and the cultural melding that took place when they arrived, Pākehā did not bring as much local cultural baggage. Māori came from communities each anchored in its rohe. Not all of this culture could be easily transferred to the new living environment (as we saw in the discussion on urban marae). Māori who have lost contact with their tribal roots are perhaps no more surprising than Pākehā who have little connection with their, say, Yorkshire ancestry, although that distancing usually happened further back in time for Pākehā.

Urban Māori

While rural–urban drift continues, the second great migration is over and Māori are now about as urban as Pākehā, although practising a different sort of urbanisation; the Pākehā family's holiday home (or even their grandma's home) does not correspond to the whānau marae, regularly visited for extended family occasions as well for holidays. (These places are visited more often now than Metge records in the 1950s, given the greater ease of travel and ownership of cars.) Of course many Pākehā do not have an out-of-town retreat, and there are those of Māori descent with little connection to their whānau rohe. But many urban Māori have a different social relationship with the countryside.

Typically, their economic position in urban society is still at the lower end, reflecting the particularities of their transition from rural to urban living described in this chapter.

Bibliography

Easton, B.H. (1996), *In Stormy Seas*. OP, Dunedin.
Easton, B.H. (forthcoming), *Not in Narrow Seas*. MUP, Auckland.

Haami, B. (2018) *Urban Māori: The Second Great Migration*. Oratia, Auckland.

Jackson, N. (1998), *Ethnic Stratification in New Zealand: A 'Total Social Production' Approach*. Thesis, University of Waikato, Hamilton.

Kawharu, H. (1968), 'Urban Migrants and "Tangata Whenua"' in E. Schwimmer (ed.) *The Maori People in the Nineteen-Sixties*. Longman Paul, Auckland.

Metge, J. (1964), *A New Maori Migration: Rural and Urban Relations in Northern New Zealand*. Athlone Press, London.

Pool, I., A. Dharmalingham and J. Sceats (2007), *The New Zealand Family from 1840*. AUP, Auckland.

Poulson, M.F. and R.J. Johnston (1973), 'Patterns of Maori Migration', in R. J. Johnston (ed.) *Urbanisation in New Zealand*. Reed Education, Wellington.

Simmons, D.R. (1976), *The Great New Zealand Myth: A Study of the Discovery and Origin Traditions of the Maori*. A.H. & A.W. Reed, Wellington.

CHAPTER 3 | **THE END OF THE GOLDEN WE(A)THER**

The Woollen Economy

For more than a century, almost from the time of the first European settlements, wool dominated the New Zealand economy. It was not the largest production sector, but it was the largest export. It provided the foreign exchange that was vital for paying for the imports needed for the nation's high standard of living, for the investment goods it needed to grow, and to service past overseas borrowing.

Initially, except for a brief decade when gold boomed in the 1860s, wool made up more than half of the goods exported. That decreased from the 1920s — but if sheep meat, which was a part of the crossbred-sheep industry, was added to the value of the wool exports, the sheep industry continued to contribute more than 50% of exports.

At the end of 1966, the dominance of the wool-export economy came to a sudden end when the price of wool crashed by 40%. It would never recover, except for a brief period in the early 1970s.

The focus in this chapter is on how the crash affected Māori, but it will be necessary to place the event in a wider context. The effect was devastating to both the sheep sector and, because it was so important, the economy; the shock lasted for decades.

The Sheep Sector Declines

For a sheep farm previously getting two-thirds of its income from wool and a third from sheep meat, a 40% drop in the price of wool meant gross revenue fell 27%. Because costs are less flexible, the reduction in net incomes was even greater.

Such a price reduction can be thought of as an earthquake that destroys a substantial proportion (more than a quarter) of the capital value in the sheep farm, including its livestock. The necessary adjustment from the reduction in farm income and the search for new sources of revenue, such as beef, is substantial.

Māori commercial sheep farms were probably smaller than non-Māori farms, but because their income over costs were also likely to have been smaller, Māori farmers may have been more heavily hit relative to scale. (The complicating factor is the size of the debt on each farm.) In the case of subsistence farms dependent on a few sheep, there would have been a loss of cash flow, with little opportunity of recourse to bank credit to tide them over. (The next paragraph mentions the reduction in cash from employment associated with subsistence farming.)

The difference from a real earthquake is that the physical capital — pastures, fences, woolsheds, livestock — remained intact, if substantially devalued while there was no insurance. The immediate response to the reduction in cash flow was to cut back on maintenance and fertiliser, and to send sheep to the freezing works. Those Māori who were proportionally over-represented in the low-skilled workforce were initially beneficiaries of the higher slaughter rates. But in the longer run, sheep numbers fell and there was less employment. (The story is complicated by productivity improvements in sheep management, but they would have happened anyway.) Māori shearing gangs — again disproportionately represented in the total workforce — would have also lost work. (Both activities were often practised by subsistence farmers.)

Price crashes and productivity shocks, such as that which affected sheep farming in 1966, are rare but not unique. Typically, the wider economy can work through such adjustments relatively easily, though they are painful to those in the affected sector. The guess is that Māori were not especially exposed in the sheep sector as owner-farmers, but more as employee and in subsistence activities. The sheep sector was especially important in the economy as a whole and, as the next section explains, Māori were more vulnerable during the adjustment.

The Economy-wide Effect of the Wool Price Crash

While the sheep sector was not prominent in the economy as a whole, it played a critical role in generating foreign exchange. The fall in its profitability required the whole economy to adapt, especially in finding new foreign-exchange earners. It may not have seemed so at the time, but this adaptation of the external production structure for exports went reasonably well. In the mid-1960s, New Zealand exports had been one of the least diversified in the OECD economies — judged by either destination or product. By the beginning of the 1980s, New Zealand exports were near the middle of the rankings. No other OECD economy showed such a substantial external diversification during that period.

External diversification had internal consequences. Before 1966 the New Zealand economy was 'two-legged'. One leg was the export sector, almost exclusively sheep and dairy farming. Its function was to earn foreign exchange, which was siphoned back to the domestic economy — especially through the use of import controls — to generate jobs and full employment. The second leg was the import-substituting activities, most obviously manufacturing, which were protected in order to sustain employment.

The distinction no longer applied after the great diversification. Now a wider range of businesses, industries and sectors contributed directly or indirectly to the earning of foreign exchange, while there were no longer the rent surpluses from farmland to siphon off to generate jobs.

In fact, the two-legged economy was an ingenious system in which the rents on farmland were transferred from farmers — via the high prices they paid for protected products — to the economy as a whole. Because this was a transfer of rents (rather than a return on capital investment), the distortions from the protection did not reduce growth as much as many thought it should. New Zealand's economic growth record of the first two post-war decades was internationally respectable.

The rent transfer, together with a raft of other protections and interventions, gave considerable stability and, consequently, security to New Zealand's economy and citizens. At the time, this post-war economic miracle was seen as New Zealand's economy developing into one that was permanently insulated from the erratic external world. In fact, the period proved to be a temporary episode made possible by favourable external conditions — especially the price of wool. Once those conditions broke down, the possibility of progress and insulation no longer existed.

This sort of experience has not been unique to New Zealand. In the early 2010s, oil-producing economies prospered from high oil prices and there was great admiration for the economic management of the politicians and technocrats who guided it. When the oil price halved (or more), the economic performance and admiration for its leaders collapsed too. At the time of writing (2017), oil-based economies are struggling through the transition of adapting to lower prices, slowed by the hope that prices will recover.(45)

The same thing happened to New Zealand after 1966. For a long time there was unwillingness in policy circles to accept that wool prices would, except for occasional years, be permanently low and that dramatic structural change was necessary.

The required structural change was not just to the pattern of production. (Foreign-exchange earning sectors had to expand and sectors which had been over-dependent on protection and subsidisation relatively contract.) The economy also experienced a cut in its real income. How was the cut to be passed on?

Views varied. Some would argue the income cuts should be borne by those on whom they directly fall; in the case of 1966 it would have been the sheep farmers. But the farmers could argue they had been sharing their rents with the economy as a whole, so the income reduction should be accordingly shared. There is no technical value-free answer and commonly, as occurred after 1966 in New Zealand and in oil-producing economies today, the political answer was to avoid the question, hoping it would go away.

If there is no direct political intervention to share the required income reduction, tensions attempting to resolve the income deficit will break out somewhere in the economy. Most typically, the tension is inflation. All Western economies experienced high inflation in the 1970s, but New Zealand's was unusually high and continued in the 1980s, after world inflation had abated.

While inflation can be a consequence of the struggle for income shares, it cannot be resolved if all incomes are indexed to one another in order to maintain relativities, and there is no significant unemployment.[6] There were strong formal and informal linkages in the economy of the 1960s and 1970s, while protection and other measures meant they could not be broken by market forces.[7] So, after 1966 inflation boomed.

The Impact on Māori

Māori would not have been especially affected by inflation. Everyone grumbles that their income relativities suffer, but given the linkages, this is usually temporary. Those who suffer are mainly on fixed incomes, say, from pensions or interest on savings. Because their wealth was lower, Māori would have been less affected.

However, as mentioned in the previous chapter, the labour market was weakening from the wool price crash. Little attention was paid to the weakening market for unskilled and low-skilled workers. Ad-hoc measures created some jobs, but they could succeed only temporarily because they were funded by offshore borrowing. Because they were at the bottom of the labour market, Māori were more directly affected.

It was especially unfortunate that this economic restructuring was occurring at the time of peak Māori urban migration, which was predicated on the old economy. The adjustment was poorly planned, which meant little attention was paid to the needs of those who would suffer most from it. The next chapter explains what happened when the strategy unwound.

Additional Complications

In 1973, half a decade after the wool price collapse, Britain entered what became the European Union (EU). This was a shock to the New Zealand economy but it had been anticipated, with corresponding adjustments already in place, including a phasing in of the loss of markets. Indeed, by 1973 the British market was already only half as important to New Zealand exports as it had been in 1966. It seems likely that had there been no wool price crash New Zealand would have coped relatively easily, albeit not without some pain, with the British entry to the EU.

More subtly, the growing post-war affluence was making the economic control mechanisms introduced during the war increasingly effective (they had been subsequently refined but not abandoned). There was more social diversity — including Māori in the urban centres — and consumers had more choice. New Zealand had held on to the centralised approach to economic management longer than comparable rich economies. Controls became increasingly ineffective, which added to the difficulties of managing an economy that was also experiencing great external diversification. The regime of Robert

Muldoon, both Prime Minister and Minister of Finance in the late 1970s, was the last to apply such an approach. Arguably he did so more intensely than at any time since the war controls were in force. The consequence was that inflation remained high and there was heavy external borrowing. Neither was sustainable.

Bibliography

Easton, B. (1996), *In Stormy Seas*. UOP, Dunedin.
Easton, B. (forthcoming), *Not in Narrow Seas*. MUP, Auckland.
Gould, J. (1985), *The Muldoon Years: An Essay on New Zealand's Recent Economic Growth*. Hodder & Stoughton, Auckland.

CHAPTER 4 | THE SHIFT TO MORE-MARKET

Introducing Economic Liberalisation

Insofar as anything in economics is inevitable, the shift of the New Zealand to 'more-market' was. The diversification of the external sector, and the rising diversity and choice in the domestic sector, meant the centralised economic management that had evolved during World War II — and culminated in the regime that Muldoon ran — was no longer viable for an affluent, democratic society such as New Zealand.

Economic liberalisation, or the use of the decentralised market to make economic decisions (also known as 'more-market'), is a broad church: there are many ways of doing it. For the purposes of this report, it is unnecessary to detail all the options. In principle, more-market — decentralisation via the use of the market — can be supported by people at any position on the political spectrum. Suffice to observe that the 1984-elected Labour Government chose the 'neoliberal' option (known locally as 'Rogernomics'), which, to simplify, is an extreme-right-wing version of more-market.

By implementing its policies very quickly, the government impeded the formation of political coalitions that could resist the changes. As a result, policy mistakes — many of which came at great cost and had to be unwound in subsequent decades — were easily made because technical criticism of them was seen as political resistance.

The focus here is on the impact of more-market on Māori. Neoliberalism was barely sensitive to Māori concerns and, as we shall see, to the concerns of any but those at the top of the income distribution; this disproportionately excluded most Māori.

Insofar as they were concerned about such things, neoliberal thinkers assumed there would be rapid economic gains and the benefits would trickle down from those at the top to the rest of the population. This did not happen. Instead, the New Zealand economy stagnated for seven years in terms of real per-capita income. The incomes of the bottom three-quarters of the country fell.

They fell for three broad reasons. First, the labour market weakened, reducing the number of jobs for those at the bottom. Second, margins for skill increased, so wages for those at the bottom fell. Third, changes to the tax system favoured those on higher incomes.

The previous chapter pointed out that as a consequence of the fall in the wool price, real incomes had to fall on average (relative to their earlier trajectory). The effect was delayed by offshore borrowing and disguised by rising prices. The Rogernomes energetically reduced inflation and borrowing, but they left the burden of adjustment to be carried by those at the bottom of the income distribution — who were disproportionately Māori.

The Weakening Labour Market

Faced with a weakening economy, the Muldoon Government maintained or introduced various job-generating programmes to employ those at the bottom of the labour skills ladder.

The most prominent were the so-called 'make work' schemes, such as the Project Employment Programmes (PEP), which enabled (particularly public sector) employers to take on workers with their remuneration paid or subsidised by central government. Less obviously, many state-owned enterprises were directed to take on extra workers, especially in regions where employment was weak. Māori were among the beneficiaries of such schemes.

The subsidies to support the job-generating schemes were a charge on the revenue or spending of the state; the PEPs involved a direct subsidy, while the job generation of state-owned enterprises reduced the dividend the corporation paid to the state coffers or increased the subsidy the state paid them. When the Rogernomes cut these programmes, it reduced the quantity of state borrowing.

The third means of job generation for the low skilled was by protecting manufacturing, such as the clothing industry, which employed them.[8] Since 1968 there had been a sort of national agreement that protection in the form of import controls should be phased out, with the likelihood that many protected businesses would close down and the resources be employed in more productive activities elsewhere. However, faced with the weakening economy through the 1970s, governments had been reluctant to abandon the controls. The Closer Economic Relations agreement of 1983 had that effect with Australia, and some expected the consequence to be more widespread. The Rogernomes took a more rapid approach.

The theory was that as the protected industries closed down, new industries would spring up to absorb the released labour. It overlooked the fact that it is easier to close down a business than start a new one. Moreover, for the theory to work, the new businesses had to be able to employ released — often low-skilled — labour, or have the labour retrained to provide the skills the businesses needed. Neither happened.9

In summary, various policies devised to protect low-skilled labour from the adjustment to the wool price collapse and shifting technological change were abandoned. While some assistance to facilitate their re-employment was promised, little was provided.

In the background was the adjustment to the wool price crash. This especially hit rural areas, so the government's job-creation schemes were biased towards those areas — especially in forestry jobs. Māori in rural areas keenly felt the impact.

While the discussion has focused on low-skilled workers, many others with better skills became redundant too. In 1991, the unemployment rate struck an unprecedented post-war level of more than 10%.

Even more extraordinarily, over the 57-month period from October 1988 to June 1993, more than three-quarters-of-a-million workers enrolled at least once with the New Zealand Employment Service register. To give some idea of this magnitude, the average size of the labour force during the period was about 1.6 million people; the enrolled unemployed represented about 47% of that total. Caveats do exist, but a reasonable summary is that in a five-year period around half the labour force experienced (involuntary) redundancy.[10]

Of course the more skilled workers in stronger regional markets quickly found new jobs, though often with inferior pay and conditions compared to their previous employment. Others — low skilled and especially in weaker regional markets — spent months, even years, unemployed.

In fact, a fifth of the labour force experienced repeated unemployment. The average cumulative duration on the register was 59.2 weeks, with Māori averaging 68.8 weeks.

Weakening Wages

There were both institutional and market reasons for real wages falling from their levels in the early 1980s.[11] Many workers would have experienced a larger fall as they moved to less well-paid jobs, while unemployment also cut incomes.

The largest institutional change was the 1991 introduction of the Employment Contracts Act, which effectively de-unionised many workers and weakened the remaining unions. Earlier changes to wage-setting in the public sector also had an effect.

Opening product markets to increased competition (especially from imports) put pressure on employers to lower wages if they wanted to survive, while higher unemployment made workers more willing to accept them.

So, collectively, the labour force experienced higher unemployment and lower remuneration, which reduced the average take-home pay.[12]

This could have been offset by tax cuts that favoured those on low incomes. But as we shall see in the next chapter, the changes in the tax and benefit system favoured those on higher incomes. As a consequence there were even greater reductions of the household incomes of those at the lower end of the income distribution.

Active Labour Market Programmes

The chapter opened by arguing that more-market was almost inevitable and that it was not a particularly right-wing approach, although New Zealand politicians chose that extreme neoliberal option.

The issue, then, for more-market modernisers who are not so extreme, is that many of the labour market outcomes described above — including higher unemployment as the workforce relocated — would have happened if they had been in charge too. Where might they have made a difference?

One possibility was to have phased in the changes more slowly. Rogernomes would argue that had that been tried, political resistance would have prevented many of the necessary changes. On the other hand, Australia achieved a similar market liberalisation transition with less pain.

As already mentioned, less-extreme modernisers would have favoured tax changes that moderated the harshness of the market income reductions; instead the tax changes increased inequality.

A third, additional approach would have been the use of comprehensive, active labour market programmes that intervened to help the unemployed find suitable work. These include:

- employment subsidies, either in the public or private sector, directly creating jobs for the unemployed;
- public employment services, such as job centres and labour exchanges, helping the unemployed with their job search;[13]
- training schemes, such as classes and apprenticeships, helping the unemployed improve their vocational skills and hence increase their employability and employment subsidies.

Comprehensive active labour market programmes have long been prominent in the economic management policies of Scandinavian countries and on the European continent.[14] New Zealand has not been so committed. In the first decades after World War II with unusually low unemployment, it was not seen as necessary. It takes a long time to build up quality training programmes. New Zealand never really started, except when there was a panic.

When the labour market deteriorated after the 1966 wool price collapse, the government introduced employment subsidies and increased employment in state-owned enterprises. In principle, these are short-term measures designed to smooth out employment fluctuations due to the business cycle. They are ill-suited for dealing with long-term structural change, such as the collapse of a major export sector, not least because of their fiscal cost and the way they compromise productivity.

During the great labour shakeout of the late 1980s, compounded by a severe business downturn in the early 1990s, the Department of Labour's New Zealand Employment Service upgraded its employment services, no doubt easing the transition between jobs for many — but not all — workers. Again though, this approach is ill-suited for dealing with long-term structural change when particular jobs are being destroyed and particular skills become useless.

What was required, and what was not provided, were training

schemes to reskill and upskill the labour force in general, and the unemployed in particular. As the previous chapter mentioned, there was little tradition of this approach in post-war New Zealand. On the whole workers had relied on generic skills and on-the-job training. Employers were reluctant to give anything but the minimum of the latter because high labour turnover meant they were unlikely to recoup their investment as the trained left. The system of polytechnics had only been established in the 1970s and policies towards mass postsecondary education were only established in the 1990s, when New Zealand found it was behind the rest of the rich world.

It takes time to instigate an effective system of training schemes, more time than was required to address the crisis of the late 1980s and early 1990s. Extraordinarily though, in the early 1990s the government decided to restructure the apprenticeship system, in effect closing it down for a period when it was greatly needed.

More fundamentally, it can be argued New Zealand should have introduced the training schemes much earlier.[15] They would have been particularly appropriate for the urbanising Māori (and Pasifika), whose specific low-skilled experience was not particularly relevant for the high-productivity industries New Zealand hoped to develop. Were the schemes developed then, they could have been ready to be adapted for the Rogernomics-triggered rise in unemployment. Instead, many of the unskilled missed out on upskilling and, at best, subsequently had patchy employment records.

The Outcome for Māori

Any introduction of more-market was going to cause turmoil in the labour market as workers moved from businesses closing down to those which were starting up or expanding. All more-market modernisers would agree it was a great pity that the required liberalisation measures were not begun earlier in the 1970s. Because they were delayed, the changes in the 1980s and 1990s were particularly turbulent.

However, there was a gross neglect of the challenges that low-skilled workers faced, and little recognition that the new direction, of which more-market was a part, would make less use of such workers. Because of where they worked and the skills they had, Māori workers were more greatly affected than the average worker.

Meanwhile, changes in the income maintenance system (income tax and benefits) reinforced the labour market pressures on most Māori.

Bibliography

Easton, B. (1987), *Wage Flexibility, Wages, and Free Lunches.* University of Melbourne Department of Economics, Melbourne.

Easton, B. (1996), *In Stormy Seas.* UOP, Dunedin.

Easton, B. (forthcoming), *Not in Narrow Seas.* MUP, Auckland.

CHAPTER 5 |  RETRENCHING THE WELFARE STATE

In the 1935 election the majority of the Māori vote went to the Coalition Government; in 1938, it went Labour's way. In 1946, when the eminent Ngata lost the final Coalition (now National) seat, all four Māori seats were held by Labour — and it remained that way for 50 years. (In the first MMP election the five Māori seats went to New Zealand First, probably as a vote for party leader Winston Peters; also, Māori would have been disenchanted by Labour's Rogernomics drive. However, their list vote still went to Labour.)

The main reason for the 1938 switch was almost certainly the passing of the Social Security Act that year, which greatly extended the government's system of benefits. (Other factors were the alliance between the Ratana Church and Labour, sealed in 1936, and increasing economic prosperity.) While entitlement was universal in principal, initially communally owned property was often used to reduce Māori benefit income. (McClure 1998: 17–18) Because the benefits were set relative to average incomes, levels were more favourable to those on lower wages (and less to those on above-average incomes). Therefore, benefits levels were relatively more advantageous to Māori.[16]

In consolidating and setting out the principles of the previous 34 years' practice, the 1972 Royal Commission on Social Security said the social welfare system aimed to 'ensure, within limitations which may be imposed by physical or other disabilities, that everyone is able to enjoy a standard of living much like that of the rest of the community, and thus is able to feel a sense of participation in and belonging to the community'. (RCSS 1972: para 42) In effect, it recommended that benefit levels be set relative to the average standard of living.

The 1991 Measures

The benefit system came under a lot of fiscal pressure in the 1980s due to the rise in unemployment. But that was, presumably, transitory. The National Government elected in 1990 had a neoliberal agenda to retrench the welfare state.[17] Benefit levels and entitlements were dramatically cut; there were also attacks on the education, health and housing components of the welfare state.

Moreover, the lower benefit rates were to be increased only in relation to consumer prices, rather than in line with rising incomes. Now beneficiaries no longer shared in rising prosperity. This practice was followed for more than a quarter of a century. In effect, the RCSS principle of a relative benefit level was replaced by an absolute benefit level, which was lower at the time and became increasingly lower relative to market incomes.[18]

At first the change was ascribed to the neoliberal predilections of the National leadership, but there was also a practical, fiscal reason. Labour had given huge tax reductions to those on top incomes by halving the top income tax rate and removing double taxation on corporate dividends. Various fudges, such as the timing of the cuts and how they were phased in, were used to hide the fact that the cuts were partially funded by increasing the structural fiscal deficit. But this was only temporary. The incoming National Government faced the hard fact that the tax cuts had to be paid for.

It could have raised income taxes, but instead it chose to deeply cut government spending; the welfare state was a major component of that spending and hence a major target (even if it had not been anathema to neoliberals).[19] Thus National completed the process of switching income distribution to favour the rich — thereby increasing income inequality — by cutting incomes and spending power further down the income ladder.

The Employment Contracts Act and Minimum Pay Rates

But it was not just fiscal prudence and a soft spot for the rich that led to the benefit cuts, as the passing of the Employment Contracts Act 1991 showed soon afterwards. The intention was, almost explicitly — even if politicians are rarely that honest — to reduce the lowest wage levels, with the expectation that lower wages would increase employment. (There is little evidence this happened once the business-cycle recovery is allowed for.)[20] It was argued that lowering benefit levels for those seeking work would make beneficiaries more ready to take low-paid jobs, because the effect of the benefit level was to put an implicit floor at the bottom of the wage structure.[21]

The Impact on Māori

Because Māori tended to have lower pay rates, higher rates of unemployment (or non-employment) and larger families, they tended to be nearer the bottom of the income distribution and experienced a disproportionally harsher impact from income cuts compared to the average household.

An indication of just how depressed the bottom was comes from the following figures, which show the time it took for the real household incomes of various deciles (tenths) of the population to recover to the level they were at in 1984.[22]

DECILE	YEARS TO RECOVER 1984 BASE
Top	4 (1988)
Second, third and fourth from top	12 (1996)
Fifth	14 (1998)
Sixth and seventh	17 (2001)
Bottom three	20 (2004)

Source: Perry 2017, table 9.2.

In summary, those at the top of the income distribution recovered within four years, but the economic and distributional changes so depressed the remaining 90% of households that it took at least twelve years before their incomes had recovered to their 1984 level. In the case of the poorest 30%, it was 20 years.

Unfortunately the sample sizes are too small to provide secure estimates for ethnic minorities in lower deciles.[23] However, an aggregate in the report may provide some clues.

The proportion of the population below a particular poverty line averaged 13% in the 1984–88 period, before the income redistribution measures were introduced. The proportion in the 1992–1996 period below the same poverty line was 23%.[24] Therefore, numbers in poverty increased about 80% (excluding the growing population).²⁵ (Perry 2017, table F.3)

We do not know the proportions for individual ethnic groups, but the report used here estimates that in 2013 and 2014 some 26% of Māori were below a particular poverty line, in comparison to a national average of 14%.²⁶ (Perry 2017: 112) Thus the Māori rate was about 85% higher — that is, a Māori person was 85% more likely to be in poverty than the population as a whole.²⁷

However, these figures about recent poverty rates do not tell us about the relative incidence of Māori poverty in the 1984–96 period and they do not tell us whether the increase of Māori in poverty was the 80% for everyone or whether the increase was lower or higher.

Whatever the exact percentages, as a result of neoliberal changes to the economy, there was an unquestionable and marked increase in the numbers of Māori households under economic pressures.

The Implications of Economic Pressures on Households

The vast majority of households in poverty consists of families/whānau: children with their parents/guardians. The foundation for nurturing the next generation can be under severe economic pressure, creating wider social and economic consequences. Children are a nation's single most important investment — economically and socially — in its future.

Reduced incomes in such households do not just cause lower levels of spending, with consequences for diet, healthcare and matters critical to social investment such as education.²⁸ Pressured households are more likely to break down and suffer domestic violence (although that occurs in well-off households, too).

The consequences of financial pressure can have long-term effects. Poor diet and healthcare in childhood is likely to result in poorer health levels in adulthood. Educational opportunities and achievement are reduced. Aside from the quality of life for affected adults in the long term, they will have lower productivity, which is a loss to the economy as a whole. Often delinquency is more common, with the consequence of higher crime and incarceration rates.

Society will spend more on the health and justice systems while getting a lower return on its education spending. Although there is considerable effort and spending on education and health measures to minimise these effects, they are ambulances at the bottom of the cliff, not fences at the top. But the fences were in fact weakened a quarter of a century ago.[29] There are mokopuna today paying the price of that past weakening.

All this illustrates the earlier remark that children are a social investment; the nation has been underinvesting in them, and it is now paying the costs of at least 25 years of severe underinvestment. Even if the country were to reverse this failure immediately, it would still need to implement a major programme of measures to address the complex fallout from the past.[30]

Since Māori are more likely to be poor, the failure to invest in Māori whānau has been particularly pernicious — as we shall see in the second part of this book. There is no reason to assume Māori are inherently less healthy, or less intelligent than non-Māori. But the failure to invest adequately in their children has led to poor outcomes.

Indeed, one could go a step further. Earlier chapters pointed out that Māori were ill-prepared for the rural–urban migration. Little additional investment was provided to deal with that. From approximately 1990 even that was cut as wages fell and support was reduced. The consequences are evident in ongoing social failure and underachievement.

Bibliography

Easton, B. (1996) *The Commercialisation of New Zealand*. AUP, 1996.
Easton, B. (forthcoming), *Not in Narrow Seas*. MUP, Auckland.
McClure, M. (1998) *A Civilised Community: A History of Social Security in New Zealand 1898-1998*. AUP, Auckland.
Perry, B. (2017) *Household Incomes in New Zealand: Trends in Indicators of Inequality and Hardship: 1982 to 2016*. MSD, Wellington.
Royal Commission on Social Security (1972) *Social Security in New Zealand*. Government Printer, Wellington.

CHAPTER 6  THE MĀORI CORPORATES

The term 'iwi' can mean 'people' or it can mean 'tribe(s)'. Unless explicitly stated, this chapter uses the term to mean the latter. The particular focus is the 'corporates': that is, tribal entities run as businesses while incorporating Māori kaupapa.

The Treaty of Waitangi Act 1975

The Treaty of Waitangi Act, passed in 1975, had little to do with opening up the New Zealand economy to the market; it was concerned with settling longstanding Māori grievances. It gave the Treaty of Waitangi recognition in New Zealand law for the first time, and established a tribunal empowered to investigate possible breaches of Te Tiriti o Waitangi by the New Zealand government or any state-controlled body.[31]

Initially the Waitangi Tribunal could only consider breaches occurring after October 1975, when the act was passed. The minister responsible, Matiu Rata, had wanted the Tribunal to hear claims dating back to the signing of Te Tiriti o Waitangi, but it was thought there was a lack of historical evidence. In 1984, however, the fourth Labour Government extended the Tribunal's authority by giving it the power to investigate claims back to 1840.[32]

The Tribunal does not settle grievances. As a general rule its findings are declarations; the Crown is not bound to follow any recommendations but it has been rare for the Crown to ignore any findings. Treaty settlements are informed by the Tribunal reports, but the settlement process involves direct negotiation between the Crown and affected parties.

Following a major decision by the Court of Appeal on the State Owned Enterprises Act, in 1989 the government set out principles to guide its actions on matters relating to the Treaty:

- the government has the right to govern and make laws;
- iwi have the right to organise as iwi, and, under the law, to control their resources as their own;
- all New Zealanders are equal before the law;
- both the government and iwi are obliged to accord each other reasonable cooperation on major issues of common concern;
- the government is responsible for providing effective processes for the resolution of grievances in the expectation that reconciliation can occur.[33] (Department of Justice 1989)

The Treaty Settlements

While there were always specific grievances to be settled, initially some of the thinking around the general settlement process seemed to propose that since the economic status of Māori and non-Māori were very different, the settlement should aim to raise the living standards of the average Māori to the national average. This would be a huge and expensive task, and would take generations.

However, Judge Edward Taihakurei Durie, then Chairman of the Waitangi Tribunal, proposed that the need was to 'move beyond guilt [the issue of the Crown's wrongdoings and Māori grievances] and ask what can be done now and in the future to rebuild the tribes'. (Waitangi Tribunal 1987: 84) This interprets the Tiriti as between the Crown and iwi, with rangatira (chiefs and high-ranking people) signing on behalf of the iwi.

The Durie approach shifted the object of the settlement process from Māori as individuals to their iwi. There might be some disagreement as to just how much was necessary to rebuild the iwi, but it cost the Crown considerably less than remedying Māori socioeconomic inequality. Stronger iwi might, to some degree, be able to make a contribution to reducing inequality but, as we shall see, given the amount transferred to them (and given that not all deprived Māori are attached to an iwi), it would be insufficient to close the gaping difference.

Durie's proposal also redirected the nature of settlements, abandoning a 'tortious' approach — that there were legal wrongs (torts) perpetrated by the Crown for which it should compensate.

In 1994 the National Government announced a settlement policy commonly called the 'fiscal envelope'. Among its principles were:

1. The Crown explicitly acknowledges historical injustices;
2. In attempting to resolve outstanding claims the Crown should not create further injustices;
3. The Crown has a duty to act in the best interests of all New Zealanders;
4. As settlements are to be durable, they must be fair, sustainable, and remove the sense of grievance;
5. The resolution process is consistent and equitable between claimant groups;
6. Nothing in the settlements will remove, restrict or replace Maori rights under Article III of the Treaty, including Maori access to mainstream government programmes; [and]
7. Settlements will take into account fiscal and economic constraints and the ability of the Crown to pay compensation.
(Department of Justice 1994)

The government set a 'fiscal envelope' of $1 billion and proceeded to settle the general claims of the iwi, so in total they would not exceed this amount. In practice, the total has been exceeded. (There are also other claims not in the envelope.)

Each iwi was allocated a portion of the total.[34] The entity representing the iwi (typically a trust board — called here 'corporates' because the large ones, especially, behave in a very businesslike way) received an amount in cash.[35] There are no direct transfers of resources, such as land, but an iwi can use its funds to purchase available Crown resources in its rohe, facilitated by the government.

There had been earlier settlements from the 1920s, with payments in perpetuity of a fixed annual amount that were not adjusted for inflation. These proved not to be 'full and final'. The lump-sum payment gives the iwi an independence from the Crown similar to any other institution with its own capital. In principle an iwi could invest unwisely and go financially bankrupt; it would have no more redress from the Crown than a business might. Thus far, most iwi have a solid financial record.

The value of historical Treaty settlements to the end of August

2017 (that is, where legislation has been enacted) is approximately $1.8 billion from 60 completed settlements. Some 25 negotiations have signed deeds of settlement valued at $400 million but have not yet had settlement legislation enacted. There are another 39 settlements currently in negotiation.[36]

This may seem a huge amount, but over a 25-year period the outlay represents a cost to the Crown of about $65 million a year. The sum of $1.65 billion invested at 5% per annum (many would think that an unrealistically high real return) would generate income of around $80 million a year, or about $3 a week per Māori.

Including the returns from their investments and adding other iwi resources (such as from the Sealord deal, other settlements or what they had accumulated earlier), some of the larger iwi have added substantially to their initial endowment.

For instance, by March 2015 the Waikato Raupatu Lands Trust had converted its original $170 million grant into a total equity of $862 million. (Tainui 2015: 47) By far the single largest group of assents is investment properties ($582 million), although some of these are mortgaged. The net profit for the year (after tax and excluding $8 million for minority interests and from revaluations) was $75 million, a return of about 10% on the $755 million with which they began the year.[37] The profit amounted to $1120 per Tainui member, or $21.50 a week. However, the Trust paid only a sixth of this to the iwi, which, with its other activities, was able to distribute $22.3 million for education ($2.8 million), Kingitanga ($1.7 million), marae facilities ($16.7 million), and other grants ($1.1 million). The remainder of the Trust's surplus was retained, adding to equity.

The implication is that while the Trust has been strengthening the iwi, little of the benefit has gone to its members. This is most likely true for most of the successful trusts.

The Māori Economy

The iwi corporates are part of the so-called 'Māori Economy'. The summary from *Tatauranga Umanga Māori 2015*, Statistics New Zealand's annual survey of Māori Authorities, reports the following:

- Māori authorities have evolved beyond traditional land-based industries, most notably into financial and insurance services.
- At February 2014, 89% of Māori authorities were located in the

North Island, particularly the rural areas of Bay of Plenty (27%) and Waikato (21%).
- Most filled jobs in Māori authorities were in agriculture, forestry, and fishing (18%), education and training (19%), and healthcare and social assistance (16%).
- Despite the predominance of Māori authorities in the rural North Island, filled jobs were concentrated in the South Island and the Waikato in 2014.
- The asset base of Māori authorities continued to grow in 2013, up 9.1% from 2012 to reach $12.5 billion.
- Total income for Māori authorities increased $430 million (18%) from 2012, to reach $2.9 billion in 2013.
- Māori authorities in the traditional land- and sea-based industries (agriculture, forestry and fishing; and rental, hiring, and real estate services) held half of all Māori authorities' assets.
- Goods exported by Māori authorities were worth $526 million in 2014, up $16 million (3.1%) from 2013.
- Kaimoana (seafood) remained the top export commodity in 2014.
- Māori authorities exported to 58 countries in 2014, up from 54 in 2013. China was the top export partner, receiving 44% of Māori authorities' total exports.[38]
(Statistics New Zealand 2015: 7)

These numbers are not large compared to the economy as a whole. The income of $12.5 billion in 2015 can be compared with a GDP of $240 billion (5.2%); exports of $526 million are compared with a national total of $67.5 billion (7.8%). That Māori authorities export relatively more than they produce domestically is a consequence of their being more active in land- and sea-based industries.

Perhaps even more instructively, Statistics New Zealand (SNZ) reports Māori authorities have 8300 employees (some of whom will not be Māori), contrasting with a total of around 200,000 jobs filled by Māori in the entire economy.

Te Puni Kōkiri (TPK) uses a wider definition of the Māori economy, including businesses run by Māori employers and self-employed Māori. (TPK 2015) The additions are derived from the Population Census; to what extent those included would describe themselves as a 'Māori business' or are run with a Māori kaupapa is not known. (SNZ is enhancing its Business Operations Survey to allow Māori businesses to self-identify.)

The summary in TPK's report on the Māori Economy in 2013 includes the following insights [author comments in square brackets].

- GDP from Māori economy producers totalled $11 billion in 2013, which represents 5.6% of New Zealand GDP; the real growth from 2010 is estimated at 2.6% [i.e. almost 0.9% per annum; the total economy grew 6.3%].
- The largest Māori-economy contribution to GDP is the primary sector, which contributed $1.8 billion, followed by manufacturing ($1.3 billion), the hire and property rental sector ($1.3 billion), the professional services sector ($1.1 billion), the education sector ($0.9 billion), construction ($0.7 billion), and the healthcare and social assistance sector ($0.7 billion). [These are in different proportions to those in the economy as a whole.] The tourist industry, which cuts across various sectors, contributes $0.4 billion.
- The Māori-economy contribution to GDP arose from an asset base totalling $42.6 billion, which is 6.1% of the total New Zealand asset base.[39] [The asset base is larger than the share of income because the Māori economy is relatively strong in the capital-intensive primary industries and weak in the service sectors.]

The TPK report also says that, in 2013, Māori comprised 12.3% of the labour force, but 5.2% of employers, 6.3% of the self-employed, 12.3% of employees (hence 11.3% of the employed labour force) and 27% of the unemployed. [The proportions in the labour force differ from the proportions in the population mainly because of the higher proportions of younger Māori.]

Disappointingly, there is no measure of the labour employed by this Māori economy. We can be sure, however, that more Māori are employed outside the 'Māori economy' than are employed in it, and that Māori collectively contribute substantially more to total GDP than the 5.6% the Māori economy covers.

Conclusion

While Treaty settlements to iwi may be a vital part of settling some long-standing grievances, they do little to enable the bulk of the Māori population to catch up with the national averages. This is especially true given that the Māori corporates are more often rurally based than the majority of the Māori population. Nor are all Māori well attached to their iwi; some do not even recognise one.

Bibliography

Department of Justice (1989), *Principles for Crown Action on the Treaty of Waitangi*. Department of Justice, Wellington.

Department of Justice (1994), *Crown Proposals for the Settlement of Treaty of Waitangi Claims*. Department of Justice, Wellington.

Easton, B. (forthcoming), *Not in Narrow Seas*. MUP, Auckland.

Statistics New Zealand (2015), *Tatauranga Umanga Māori 2015: Updated statistics on Māori Authorities*. Statistics NZ, Wellington.

Tainui: Waikato Raupatu Lands Trust (2015), *Annual Report: Financial Statements*. Tainui: Waikato Raupatu Lands Trust, Hamilton.

Te Puni Kōkiri (2015), *Te Ohanga Māori 2013: Māori Economy Report 2013*. Te Puni Kōkiri, Wellington.

Waitangi Tribunal (1987), *Waiheke Tribunal Report*; Wai 10. Waitangi Tribunal, Wellington.

CHAPTER 7 | **MĀORI COMMUNITY RESPONSES**

Traditionally the term 'whānau' referred to what anthropologists call 'extended family'. However, recently it has been used to refer to a Māori community that need not be a kinship group. For instance, the Māori urban authority in West Auckland (Waipareira) calls itself 'Te Whānau o Waipareira'. Its first noun refers to 'extended family' only in a very wide sense of 'extended', and may better be translated as 'community'. Unless it is very clear that the term 'whānau' is being used to mean 'extended family', this chapter uses it to mean a community of Māori with only very loose kinship ties. If the previous chapter was about 'iwi' as tribes, this one is about 'iwi' as people.

Many of the urbanised Māori, in centres where their iwi reach was weak, retained only a loose attachment to their iwi. Traditional means of expressing Māoriness — living as a Māori — were diminished; urban-born descendants of the migrating generation had even weaker connections.

For instance, the marae was central to traditional (and therefore rural) Māori culture and community activities. Those who left their rural marae for the city were not tangata whenua in their urban locations and so were not strictly entitled to have a marae of their own. Instead they were 'manuhiri' on the marae of the tangata whenua, a status similar to Pākehā (although inter-iwi/tribal kinship ties could moderate this status).

Such urbanised Māori were likely to lose their roots without some sort of urban equivalent of a marae, with its community and sense of a place where they could stand in their own right. Commonsense and Māori adaptability prevailed; initially, 'pan-tribal' or 'national' urban marae accommodated those who were not tangata whenua. Nowadays, many living in the cities have established marae outside their tribal boundaries.[40] However, the buildings and land are not always in the form of traditional marae, and they may be used for other purposes such as Te Kōhanga Reo (Māori-language-immersion early childhood education — Māori language nests).

So rather than lose contact with their Māori roots, many Māori joined pan-Māori alternative institutions that have evolved outside the traditional iwi strictures.

Māori Women's Welfare League

The Māori Women's Welfare League is the oldest of the institutions covered in this chapter. Inevitably, the League was primarily based in rural areas at first but it followed the urban migration and is now active in urban centres too.

The League was founded in 1951 because women were under-represented in existing Māori institutions, which tended to be preoccupied with male issues. Initially the League was heavily involved in housing, health and education, focusing on families and healthy lifestyles in addition specific to women's issues. Subsequently the scope evolved to pay greater attention to the needs of urban Māori women. An important initiative in which the League was involved (but not uniquely) was the founding of Te Kōhanga Reo.

Gangs

Urban Māori gangs seem to be an indigenous way of creating social units in the cities.[41] The first gang was established in the 1960s: a relatively early stage in post-war Māori urbanisation, but not at the beginning of urbanisation. The gangs are seen as the product of the breakdown of whānau links in the cities for the children and grandchildren of those Māori who had migrated. (Waitangi Tribunal 1998: 36)

Unfortunately there is little balanced commentary or research on gangs (Gilbert 2013 is a notable exception). Public attitudes are dominated by the fact that gangs are most likely to grab headlines when they're associated with violence or criminal activity. When gangs are peaceful and going about lawful activities, they hardly come to public attention.

Māori Urban Authorities

The rapid post-war urbanisation created a series of challenges for urban dwellers, ranging from the breakdown of traditional whānau links to meeting responsibilities such as mortgage payments (not a major issue in subsistence Māoridom) and facing alcohol abuse. These would be intensified from the late 1960s by the weakening of the labour market. (Waitangi Tribunal 1998: 35–36)

One of the chief responses was through Māori committees established under the Māori Welfare Act 1962. The committees were the most 'grass-roots' level in a system of non-tribal Māori associations that included Māori executive committees, district Māori councils, and the New Zealand Māori Council.

The committees covered a wide range of activities including promoting tikanga Māori, te Reo, business, horticulture, health, education and other social needs in a holistic way. They could be innovative, initiating family group conferences in the mid-1970s — well before they became formalised in law under the Children, Young Persons, and Their Families Act 1989. They established urban, or pan-tribal, marae. (Waitangi Tribunal 1998: 37)

The plethora of overlapping organisations in a large region often led to a tortuous consolidation into an Urban Māori Authority. The first was Te Whānau o Waipareira, which was constituted under the Charitable Trusts Act 1957 in 1984. (Waitangi Tribunal 1998: 37–38) It provides the wider West Auckland community with a one-stop location for health, social, justice and education services, plus budgeting, recruitment and tax advice. While nominally pan-Māori, it will also provide services to non-Māori.[42]

Others include the Manukau Urban Māori Authority (South Auckland), Te Rūnanga o Kirikiriroa Trust (Hamilton), Te Rūnanganui o Te Ūpoko o Te Ika (Wellington), and Te Rūnanga o Ngā Maata Waka (Christchurch).[43] Typically each has a significant asset base, but its main revenue comes from public sources — ultimately the central government. (This is discussed further in the conclusion, p. 61.)

In an important decision, the Waitangi Tribunal ruled in 1988 that significant pan-Māori community providers, such as Te Whānau o Waipareira, are Treaty partners; partnership was not confined to iwi or kinship groups. (Waitangi Tribunal 1998: 221) This is an acknowledgement, also made in other Tribunal findings, that Māori have a right to develop and evolve with changing circumstances — their urbanisation has been a major one. The principle applies not just to the particular trust that brought the claim, but to all such providers and, indeed, to all such pan-Māori organisations.

Māori Health Promotion Agencies

While iwi, and Urban Māori Authorities and their equivalents, provide preventative health care where they operate, there is a need for national health promotion campaigns and advocacy. However, there can be parallel Māori national agencies such as Hāpai te Hauora.

Their importance is that these agencies can address the issues informed by and sensitive to Māori cultural perspectives, including going where Pākehā would be reluctant. For instance, despite Māori having one of the highest rates of smoking in the world, only a Māori-dominated institution could acceptably propose that marae be smokefree.

Māori Broadcasting

As part of the settlement over te Reo Māori and the radio frequency spectrum claims (Wai 11, 26, 150), the government established and continues to fund Te Māngai Pāho (Māori Broadcast Funding Agency), which is responsible for promoting Māori language and culture by providing funding for Māori language programming, on radio and television and for popular music.

This has enabled the establishment of a free-to-air Māori television channel and a network of 21 bilingual (English and Māori) radio stations. (Although they are described as 'iwi radio stations', not all are tribal; many are located in provincial cities.)

Whānau Ora

Whānau Ora (Family Wellbeing) is an inclusive approach to providing services and opportunities to communities across New Zealand. It empowers whānau as a whole, rather than focusing separately on individual members and their problems.

Launched in 2010 and administered by Te Puni Kōkiri, Whānau Ora brings together services normally delivered by a number of government agencies, from Te Puni Kōkiri to the Ministry of Health and the Ministry of Social Development. Instead, Māori community agencies such as iwi or Urban Māori Authorities deliver the services using a more holistic approach. The aim is to align central government funding and regulation with the Māori agencies delivering the services.

Conclusion

Through a range of institutions such as those described in this chapter, many urban Māori have been able to maintain cultural connections, whether they were otherwise disconnected from their iwi (tribe) or unable to connect with it because they lived out of the rohe. Not all disconnected Māori use the institutions, but those who do have kept more in contact with their cultural roots than was otherwise possible. What will eventually happen to their descendants, and the role of iwi in Māori life, only time will tell.

One common feature of almost all the institutions described here is their dependence upon regular funding from government — in contrast to the iwi corporates from the previous chapter, which have built on the capital restitutions to create independent income arising from their investments.

Imagine that at some future date, New Zealand has a strongly neoliberal government that slashes government spending.[44]

We may argue what the likely effect of spending cuts and the accompanying tax cuts on household budgets would be. In my judgement, the likely outcome would be that poorer Māori households would suffer greatly. Less questionably, Māori community organisations would experience drastic cuts to their budgets and have to reduce the services they provide. Many would have to close down; the remainder would struggle.[45]

The neoliberal theory is that, with greater cash income, households would be able to purchase the services from market suppliers that they currently receive from Māori community organisations.[46] Even so, the individualistic delivery would undermine the community ethic and so inhibit those of Māori descent from expressing their Māoriness. The Waitangi Tribunal might well rule that this was a breach of the obligations set out in the Treaty.

While the above scenario is, in my judgement, unlikely, it underlines the critical dependence that the community organisations have on central government funding.

But there is another lesson. The shift to more-market in the 1980s and 1990s reduced the quantity of services — educational, health, social welfare and other such services — supplied by central government. The supply gap has been replaced by profit and non-profit organisations that receive funding from central government for the services they provide. This 'outsourcing' made possible the rise of the strong Māori community organisations described in this chapter. One consequence of the shift from central supply was that local supply could be more responsive to local needs, including enabling those of Māori descent to maintain connections with cultural roots.

Bibliography

Douglas, R. (1993) *Unfinished Business*. Random House, Auckland.

Easton, B. (forthcoming) *Not in Narrow Seas*. MUP, Auckland.

Gilbert, J. (2013), *Patched: The History of Gangs in New Zealand*. VUP, Wellington.

Waitangi Tribunal (1986), Report of the Waitangi Tribunal on the Te Reo Māori Claim: Wai 11. Waitangi Tribunal, Wellington.

Waitangi Tribunal (1990), Report of the Waitangi Tribunal on Claims Concerning the Allocation of Radio Frequencies: Wai 26 and Wai 150. Waitangi Tribunal, Wellington.

Waitangi Tribunal (1998), *Te Whānau o Waipareira Report:* Wai 414. Waitangi Tribunal, Wellington.

CHAPTER 8 | **MĀORI TODAY**

This chapter provides a narrative that synthesises the statistics in Part Two, and begins with a non-quantitative summary of their conclusions.

Being Māori
Around 15% of New Zealanders say they are of Māori ethnicity. About 70% say Māori culture is important or somewhat important to them. About a quarter speak te Reo at least fairly well, and another tenth say they understand the Māori language, so they are able to follow a conversation in te Reo even if they cannot join in.

Demography
Māori comprise 14–15% of the population on an ethnic basis and 15–16% of the population on a descent (genealogy) basis. The urban migration is largely over, but Māori differ from the overall population by being younger and because their numbers are growing faster.

Educational Achievement
At the age of 15, Māori students are on average educationally behind Pākehā; about a quarter of them have not reached educational levels that enable them to function competently in society. Not surprisingly this weakness is transmitted into low skills when they are adults, and they have fewer (or lower) qualifications. The consequence is, on average, Māori have inferior employment opportunities and lower incomes compared to Pākehā.

Employment
Unemployment is effectively much higher among Māori than is generally realised, if those discouraged from seeking work are included. Māori tend to be in low-skilled occupations, although there appears to have been some improvement over time. Māori tend to be more in the primary sector and tourism, but not as frequently as is generally thought, and there are other industrial sectors where Māori are more intensively employed.

Health
Māori have poorer health, as measured by mortality and independent life expectancy. They live fewer years and have poorer-quality health during those years. While there was some catch-up in the post-war era, there has been relative stagnation in recent years, and in the case of Māori men some evidence of regression.

Incomes
Māori incomes are lower than those of Pākehā. Their earnings are lower, and Māori male earnings are relatively lower than those of Māori females. They have lower levels of investment income, while government transfers such as social security do not offset the overall deficit. There is no evidence of trends in the relativities of market incomes: Māori market incomes are below the Pākehā ones, but the evidence over the last two decades — as far back as we can go — shows the gap is neither increasing nor decreasing. In regard to (equivalised) household (disposable) incomes, today's Maori relativity with Pākehā seems to have fallen markedly as a result of the neoliberal redistributional policies of the late 1980s and early 1990s, but has been fairly stable since 1996.

The Criminal Justice System
Māori are over-represented in the criminal justice system (including as victims of crimes). A Department of Corrections report identifies small biases operating within the criminal justice system, resulting in an accumulation of individuals within that system. A range of adverse early-life social and environmental factors put Māori at greater risk of ending up in patterns of adult criminal conduct. Ultimately the accounts of Māori over-representation in the criminal justice system — and, indeed, of over-representation in poor economic outcomes —

involve a process of cumulative circular causation through time. One event influences subsequent events, both for the individual and future generations.

Wealth and Housing

The available fragmentary evidence is that Māori have much lower net worth than Pākehā, not all of which can be explained by their being earlier in the life — and therefore wealth — cycle. One consequence is that Māori experience inferior housing, which affects their wellbeing, health and prospects.

Māori Today

By the beginning of the 21st century, Māori had completed their urban migration and the more-market economic regime had settled in. Some had expected that those who grew up in the urban centres after the migration would fully adapt to urban living, becoming much like the Pākehā already living there. Three and four generations later, that has not happened for many urban Māori.

The difference does not lie in the fact that many Māori have continued to celebrate their culture (to be fair, many non-Māori also celebrate Māori culture). On a whole range of social indicators such as education, employment, income and criminal justice, Māori themselves judge that their people are not doing well.

What the early optimists overlooked was the difficulty of the urban transition and the need for extra measures and policies to enable Māori to adjust to urban life — in addition to making up for the deficit that rural Māori already faced. Initiatives were introduced but half-heartedly; many were abandoned under the extreme neoliberal version of a more-market regime. Māori, and others who were less advantaged, not only suffered a direct set-back from the changes, but the failure to provide compensating measures or reinstate successful past ones meant the adjustment slowed down, stagnated and even reversed.

On a personal note, this writer has been monitoring Māori economic progress on social indicators for four decades. At first, the overall pattern of steady incremental relative gains suggested Māori would eventually catch up to Pākehā — although 'eventually' would certainly have not been before the middle of this century, more than 100 years after the great urban migration began. However, the inventory of indicators in Part Two suggests the steady incremental gains are no longer happening. Apparently, for a decade or more, there have been no marked gains. Instead there has been stagnation and even some setbacks.

Māori education and employment levels remain below those of Pākehā with little evidence of catching up, while the evidence points to Māori household incomes as not only markedly lower than non-Māori ones, but growing more slowly than the national average. Arguably, the growth deficiency — of about 3.5 percentage points a decade — is small, but the gap is widening.

What is happening? The simple answer is that social security benefit levels were not indexed to prosperity but, except for the April 2016 increase in family support, have been maintained at the same real level as they were set in 1990 (that is, adjusted only for inflation), which was not very different from the level the Royal Commission on Social Security judged inadequate in 1972. Others have benefited from growing prosperity since then; social security beneficiaries have not.[47]

However, the stagnation of real benefit levels is not a sufficient explanation of deteriorating relative incomes. The neoliberal justification, such as it was, for the benefit cuts and stagnation was that this would create more employment and higher wages. So the theory — poorly articulated and perhaps hardly hypothesised — was that while government transfers might stagnate, the new market environment would generate higher incomes in total for those at the bottom of the income distribution.

However, as Part Two demonstrates, that did not happen to Māori relative to non-Māori; there was no convergence of incomes, and income inequality increased. The details of why it did not happen — why the neoliberal account is out of touch with the realities of the labour market (and indeed the education market) — need not detain us. That it happened is established in the outcomes recorded in Part Two.

Moreover, the gloomy prophecy is that there is not likely to be a major change in the indicators under the current circumstances, including the current policy regime.

It is not the task of this work to suggest alternative policies, so instead it concludes by looking at some contemporary issues raised by Part Two: Māori are a more complex heterogeneous entity than the single term to describe them might suggest. Of course, that is true for all social groups, but Part Two draws out a couple of issues worth pondering because they may have wider implications.

The first is that, while in an obvious sense men and women are different, on the indicators reported in Part Two, Māori women are more like non-Māori women than Māori men are like non-Māori men. The fact is open to a number of interpretations; we need more data before choosing one. The immediate practical issue is that collected statistics need to provide gender specifics more often than they do.

The second issue arises because individuals sometimes categorise themselves as belonging to more than one ethnicity: for instance, 'Māori' and 'Pākehā'. The statisticians' tendency has been either to prioritise, so Māori-Pākehā are classified as 'Māori', or to double-count, so Māori-Pākehā are classified as both 'Māori' and 'Pākehā' and the total exceeds the numbers of individuals. Neither is satisfactory. When it was possible to distinguish them, Māori-Pākehā proved to have different characteristics from sole-Māori and on some, but not all, measures were similar to sole-Pākehā. (When they are not, they seem to 'average' between sole-Māori and sole-Pākehā.) Again, an improvement in the statistical base would be to separate them out for comparative analysis purposes.[48]

The last two paragraphs are from the perspective of a social statistician, but if more attention was given to them they may tell a deeper story that would enrich this book's narrative. Examining why Māori women have a different history may tell us more about the Māori experience, and/or possibly women's experience; the rise of what appears to be, in effect, a new and substantial ethnicity (Māori-Pākehā), more prosperous than sole-Māori, may help us understand strategies for improving the lot of the latter.[49]

To conclude, Māori made a brave new migration after the war from country to town. They began with a disadvantage that was only slowly addressed by public policies. However, many of the policies and the economic forces they supported were swept away by the neoliberal more-market revolution of the late 1980s and early 1990s. As a result, the incremental gains seem to have slowed down, even stagnating or reversing.

The hope had been that, some time this century, Māori would move much closer to Pākehā when compared using the various social and economic indicators. Here the author must conclude that on recent policies, such an outcome seems unlikely. Yet the evidence shows Māori as a social group is likely to survive. Whether the nation accepts these long-term disparities as inevitable, or takes action to moderate the policies and processes causing stagnation and regression, will determine the actual outcome.

Bibliography

Easton, B. (forthcoming) *Not in Narrow Seas.* MUP, Auckland.

Haami, B. (2018) *Urban Māori: The Second Great Migration.* Oratia, Auckland.

PART TWO

The following chapters provide the statistical background that informs the preceding narrative, especially chapter 8.

'Pākehā' is used rather than 'European' because the latter can only have a racial interpretation. Non-Māori includes Pasifika, Asians and others. The Māori-Pākehā comparison is preferred because it avoids some particularisers of each of the other ethnic groups.

Statistical Accuracy

Aside from the Population Census, the statistics reported here are derived from samples and are subject to sampling errors — as are all projections and trends. It is always necessary to be cautious in such circumstances. In the case of sub-groups of a sample, the sampling errors are necessarily proportionally larger.

CHAPTER 9 | **BEING MĀORI**

What it means to be Māori cannot be easily captured by a statistician. However, a couple of indicators are the ability to speak Māori, and responses when asked the importance of Māori culture. A fundamental problem for the statistician is how people describe themselves.

Defining Māori

The definition of Māori in statistical records has varied over the years, which makes longitudinal comparisons complicated, and can add ambiguity to an analysis. There are at least two distinct definitions: 'objective' and 'subjective'.

A person with at least one Māori ancestor is objectively of Māori descent, a status that can be assessed unambiguously.[50] It is the definition used for entitlement to register on the Māori electoral roll and the response to a question asked in the New Zealand Population Census.[51]

Thus, Peter Robinson exhibits as a Māori artist, although only one of his great-great-great-grandparents was Māori (Ngāi Tahu). He happily admits his marginal status, as evidenced in his series *Percentage Paintings*. (By a conventional measure, 'bloodline', he is one thirty-second, or 3.125%, Māori.)

But there is a second way in which Robinson is Māori. He acknowledges it. He could have been of Māori descent but said it meant nothing to him. (Āpirana Ngata had a Scottish grandfather and said his Pākehā ancestry was the source of his methodical habits, but otherwise he did not regard it as important.) That is true for some of Māori descent, and is complicated by adopting a different status at various stages in their life or in different circumstances. It can lead to misleading data. For instance, a person may say they are Māori in the Population Census but may not be so recorded in their death registration or for some other official purpose.

This second, subjective, assignment of Māori, is also asked in the Population Census in a question on ethnicity.[52] Most of Māori descent say they are ethnically Māori, but about half report another ethnicity (or two) as well.

Moreover, subjective ethnicity is a very fluid phenomenon, varying with circumstances.[53] This is a persistent problem in the surveys reported here. A common statistical response is to rebase the survey results so the ethnicity proportions are those reported by the Census population.

Where it is necessary to make the distinction, this book uses 'Māori descent' (rather than 'objectively Māori') and 'Māori ethnicity' (rather than 'subjectively Māori').

Language/Te Reo

Te Kupenga (the Māori Social Survey) is a sample survey of the usually resident New Zealand population, aged 15 years and older, who identify with Māori ethnicity and/or are of Māori descent.[54] Responses are shown in Table 9.1.

Table 9.1: Ability to Speak Te Reo, Māori Aged Over 15, 2013 (percentage)

	FEMALE	MALE
Very well/well	12.1	9.1
Fairly well	13.3	10.4
Not very well	32.9	31.2
No more than a few words/phrases	41.5	49.3
TOTAL including don't know/refused	100	100

Source: Statistics New Zealand (2014)

A little less than a quarter of those with Māori ethnicity say they can speak te Reo very well, well or fairly well; women are more fluent than men. The proportion rises a little with age; the oldest are also more likely to report they speak with greater fluency in the very well and well category.[55]

There is also a question on respondents' understanding of Māori. About a third of the group said they understood very well, well or fairly well, so there are about (another) 10% who say they are able to follow a conversation in te Reo even if they cannot join in.

Importance of Māori Culture

Te Kupenga also asked how important Māori culture was to respondents. Their responses are shown in Table 9.2.

Table 9.2: Importance of Māori Culture, Māori Aged Over 15, 2013 (percentage)

	FEMALE	MALE
Very important	26.3	21.5
Quite important	22.1	22.3
Somewhat important	24.3	24.3
A little important	18.5	20.8
Not at all important	9.1	10.9
TOTAL including don't know/refused	**100**	**100**

Source: Statistics New Zealand (2014)

Almost half (46.1%) of those of Māori ethnicity consider Māori culture is 'very' and 'quite' important to them; add those who think it is somewhat important and the proportion is close to 70%. Women are slightly more likely to think so than men. There appears to be little difference in the proportion by age.

Four-fifths (80%) of those who speak te Reo very well, well or fairly well consider Māori culture is very important or quite important to them. However, only 36% of those who think Māori culture is very important or quite important can speak the language very well, fairly well, or well. The implication is that fluency in te Reo need not be central to an individual's commitment to Māori culture — but it helps. There appear to be no differences in the proportions by age.

Conclusion

At first glance, some of the results in this chapter are puzzling. Just over a quarter of those who claim Māori ethnicity think Māori culture is only a little important to them or less. Perhaps many respond to the ethnicity question by answering in terms of race or descent. We do not know how many tick Māori only or how many tick other ethnicities in this survey.

On the other hand, while te Reo is central to Māori culture, it is evident that many committed to the culture are far from fluent speakers.

Bibliography

Statistics New Zealand (2014), *Te Kupenga 2013*. Statistics NZ, Wellington.

CHAPTER 10 | DEMOGRAPHY

In the 2013 Census, 668,724 people (15.8% of all respondents) said they were of Māori descent; 598,605 people (14.1%) identified with the Māori ethnic group, of which 320,406 people (or 53.3% of all ethnic Māori) identified with two or more ethnic groups.

Numbers

The 1951 Census reported there were 134,097 Māori in New Zealand. Six decades later, in 2013, the Census counted 668,724. This covers only those in New Zealand on Census night. There will be New Zealand-based Māori on overseas travel and some permanently based overseas. Demographer Tahu Kukutai thinks about one-fifth of all Māori in the world now live outside New Zealand, most of them in Australia. (Collins 2012)

Including those Māori overseas, the yearly population growth over the 62 years amounted to about 2.8%. This is higher than one could expect in a closed population but, of course, Māori may have children with non-Māori people who are of (some would say 'partial') Māori descent and may take on a Māori ethnicity.

Māori fertility was about seven children per woman in the 1940s and 1950s, but fell rapidly in the 1960s to just above two by the 1970s: close to the non-Māori rate and the population replacement rate. Internationally experienced demographer Ian Pool says it was the fastest fall he had witnessed. He explained the decline as fitting all the hallmarks of classic demographic transition theory: massive urbanisation, increased survivorship (especially of babies), universal exposure to Western education, changing cultural ideology, and the availability of efficient contraception (sterilisation was more common than the pill for Māori). (Pool 1991: 170–75)

Even so, in future the Māori population will grow as a proportion of the total population, subject to the caveat of excluding growth from migration. First, on current definitions a child of a Māori and non-Māori is likely to be classified as Māori (the child may also be classified with another ethnicity). Second, Māori women have their children younger so over the years Māori have more generations than non-Māori.

While this puts Māori population growth at an 'advantage', it puts many Māori women at a career disadvantage since the standard pattern for Pākehā women is to hold off having children — often until they're in their thirties, until after they have established a career.

Current 'median' (middle) projections suggest that in 2038 (as far out as Statistic New Zealand projects), the proportion of the population with Māori ethnicity will be 19.5%, compared to the 14.1% who said so in the 2013 Population Census. Inevitably the projections are fraught with assumptions that may not occur: critically, that current practices of identifying ethnicity will continue, and that migration will continue with a similar pattern to that of the past decade.

The proportions for the three other projected ethnicities are: Asian, 20.4% in 2038 (up from 12.2% in 2013);[56] Pasifika, 10.9% (up from 7.8%); and European or Other (including New Zealander), 65.6% (down from 74.6%). The total adds up to 116.9% (up from 110.2%) because of the current practice to record those with multiple ethnicities as multiple people.

Gender Balance

As Table 10.1 shows, the male-to-female ratio varies by age.

There are more females than men in New Zealand, among Māori and the total population. However, at birth and up to the late teenage years, the number of males is higher. The subsequent switch from the 20s reflects higher mortality and (probably) higher outward migration. There does not seem to be much evidence from the table that Māori of different ages had different ethnicity choices, since the descent pattern is broadly the same.

Table 10.1: Males per 1000 Females, 2013

AGE RANGE	MĀORI		ALL POPULATION
	DESCENT	ETHNICITY	
Under 5	1060	1051	1046
5–14	1048	1052	1043
15–24	948	968	1023
25–64	833	846	921
65 and over	819	817	850
TOTAL	**920**	**931**	**948**

Source: Statistics New Zealand, 2013 Population Census

Fertility

Fertility is defined as the actual level of reproduction of a population based on the number of live births that occur, and is usually measured by births in a women's lifetime. It is complicated at the ethnic level[57] because part of a child's ethnicity may be derived from the father, and not just the mother, while he or she may have multiple ethnicities.[58]

A baby's ethnicity tends to reflect the ethnicities of both parents. In 2010, 74% of births registered belonged to only one ethnic group, 22% belonged to two ethnic groups, and 3% belonged to three ethnic groups. Just over half as many mothers (14%) as babies (26%) identified with more than one ethnic group.

The total fertility for the Māori ethnic group in the December 2010 year was 2.8 births per woman, compared to 1.9 among Pākehā and well above replacement level (2.1 births per woman). However, this should not be taken to mean the number of children of sole-Māori ethnicity is growing rapidly. In the December 2010 year, 69% of Māori babies belonged to two or more ethnic groups. (In contrast, 67% of Pākehā babies belonged to only one ethnic group.)

While the fertility rates for Māori mothers under 25 years of age were more than double the fertility rates for the total populations in the same age groups, they were lower in the 30–39 age range. (The fertility rate for the Māori population was higher than the rate for the total population in all age groups above 40 years of age.)

Mortality

Mortality is (implicitly) covered in chapter 13, which looks at life expectancy, which is derived by aggregating mortality. Since Māori life expectancy is shorter, their mortality ratios are higher, but the margin differs by age.

Locations

Table 10.2 demonstrates the share of Māori population by regional council areas.

Table 10.2: Proportions of Total Māori By Region

REGIONAL COUNCIL AREA	2001 CENSUS PERCENTAGE	2013 CENSUS PERCENTAGE
Auckland	24.3	23.8
Waikato	13.8	14.0
Bay of Plenty	12.1	11.5
Wellington	9.7	9.7
Northland	7.7	7.5
Manawatu-Whanganui	7.5	7.3
Hawke's Bay	6.1	5.8
Canterbury	6.0	7.0
Gisborne	3.7	3.1
Taranaki	2.8	3.0
Otago	2.0	2.4
Tasman-Nelson-Marlborough*	1.8	2.1
Southland	1.9	1.9
West Coast	0.5	0.5
Total New Zealand**	**100**	**100**

Source: Statistics New Zealand, 2013 Population Census; rounding may mean columns do not add up to a precise total.
* Three small regions combined.
** Includes those outside regional council areas.

Table 10.3 gives the proportions for selected territorial authorities.[59]

While there remains a preponderance of Māori in their traditional areas in the north, they are steadily diffusing through the entire country with a slight drift south — especially to the South Island, perhaps as Māori move towards the national pattern of locations. The majority of Māori live in the four largest urban areas.

The tables show a great deal of stability over the 12-year period. However, the overall story is that the urbanisation is largely completed (unless the external shift to Australia is treated as an extension of internal urban migration).

Table 10.3: Proportions of Total Māori By Selected Territorial Authorities

TERRITORIAL AUTHORITIES	2001 CENSUS PERCENTAGE	2013 CENSUS PERCENTAGE
Auckland*	24.3	23.8
Wellington Urban Authorities*	8.7	8.7
Hamilton City*	4.2	4.8
Christchurch City*	4.3	4.6
Napier City-Hastings District*	4.5	4.5
Rotorua District*	4.1	3.7
Northland District	4.1	3.7
Gisborne District	3.7	3.3
Whangarei District*	2.9	3.1
Tauranga District*	2.7	3.1
Total of Above	**63.5**	**63.3**
Total of Urban Above	**55.7**	**56.3**

Source: Statistics New Zealand, 2013 Population Census; rounding may mean columns do not add up to a precise total.
* Only or predominantly urban.

Age

To understand the current state of Māori and their prospects, it is critical to recognise the difference in the age structure between them and the whole population (shown in Table 10.4).

Māori are younger. Half of them are under the age of 25: half of the rest of the population are over the age of 40. The difference arises partly from Māori mothers being younger than non-Māori mothers, but also because of the effect of children born to two ethnicities (probably) being assigned to both.

The two populations have different demands on the public sector. Māori have a relatively greater impact on education and family support services, and non-Māori (generally) on services for older people. To illustrate, there is a grumble that Māori have unusually high demands on the social welfare system, but that is characteristic of the young; Māori demands on New Zealand Superannuation are relatively much lower.

Table 10.4: Proportions in Age Groups, Māori and Total Populations, 2013

AGE GROUP YEARS	MĀORI POPULATION PERCENTAGE	NEW ZEALAND POPULATION PERCENTAGE
0–9	23.1	13.6
0–19	20.5	13.7
20–29	14.3	12.9
30–39	11.7	12.4
40–49	12.2	14.3
50–59	9.7	13.2
60–69	5.4	10.1
70 and over	3.2	9.7
Total	100	100

Source: Statistics New Zealand, 2013 Population Census; rounding may mean columns do not add up to a precise total.

Bibliography

Collins, S. (2011), '18 Per Cent of Maori Now Live Overseas', *New Zealand Herald*, 29 November 2011.

Pool, D.I. (1991), *Te Iwi Maori*. AUP, Auckland.

Statistics New Zealand (2012), *Ethnicity and Crowding: a Detailed Examination of Crowding among Ethnic Groups in New Zealand 1986–2006*. Statistics NZ, Wellington.

Statistics New Zealand (various years), *Population Census*. Statistics NZ, Wellington.

CHAPTER 11  **EDUCATIONAL ATTAINMENT**

The ability to statistically identify educational attainment is more limited than at first might be expected. This chapter looks at three different measures.

Years of Highest Educational Qualification

Table 11.1 shows the 2006 Census reported the average highest educational qualification (weighted by years) held by the ethnic groups labelled Pākehā and Māori.[60] For simplicity in identifying cohorts, it is assumed the Census was taken on 1 January 2006.

The scores can be roughly interpreted as years beyond a zero qualification.[61] Thus, in 2006, Pākehā aged 15–19 years — say, 17.5 year-olds — had on average obtained 1.6 qualification years, while Māori had attained only 1.3 years.

Interpreting the data is a little tricky because the age categories are cohorts and younger cohorts tend to obtain more qualifications than older ones. The table is not implying that 35–39 year-olds lose qualifications in their next five years. Rather, it is saying those born between 1966 and 1970 are better qualified than those born five years earlier.

More subtly, it is evident from the table that individuals continue to acquire significant qualifications long after early adulthood. The data suggests this is a major phenomenon at least until people reach their early forties.

Critically for our purposes, Māori qualification attainment is markedly below Pākehā attainment; typically by more than a year after the age of 20, and rising to a year and a half later in life.

Table 11.1: Highest Educational Qualification by Age and Ethnicity (measured in years after no qualification: average)

COHORT (BIRTH YEAR)	AGE	PĀKEHĀ	MĀORI	DIFFERENCE
1986–90	15–19	1.6	1.3	0.3
1981–85	20–24	3.5	2.4	1.1
1976–80	25–29	4.2	2.6	1.6
1971–75	30–34	4.4	2.8	1.6
1966–70	35–39	4.4	2.9	1.5
1961–65	40–44	4.0	2.7	1.3
1956–60	45–49	3.7	2.4	1.3
1951–55	50–54	3.6	2.4	1.2
1946–50	55–59	3.5	2.2	1.3
1941–45	60–65	3.1	2.0	1.1
Before 1941	65+	2.5	1.5	1.0

Source: Statistics New Zealand. *NZ Stats* 2006

How important is that difference? One way of thinking about it is that, roughly, a Māori at the age of 40 had a similar qualification attainment level to a Pākehā at the age of 60. In effect Māori attainment is two decades — almost a generation — behind Pākehā attainment. A Māori born in, say, 1985 will have, on average, parents with a qualification level similar to that of the grandparents of the Pākehā born in the same year.

This has long-term implications and works against Māori getting a Pākehā-equivalent education — although many Māori have overcome these handicaps (as have Pākehā in similar circumstances), often with the support of their parents.

This is but one glimpse we have into the data of how family situations shape educational attainment and subsequent opportunity. Regrettably, other than anecdote, there is little else in the way of evidence.

Adult Skills

The latest Adult Skills Survey (2014), which is part of the OECD Programme for the International Assessment of Adult Competencies (PIAAC), is not fully analysed, but what is available is useful. The headline conclusion is that 'there are significant skill differences between ethnic groups'; Māori prove to be behind Pākehā and Asian, but Pasifika are even further behind. Table 11.2 summarises the differences.

The reported numerical level and hence the numerical differences by themselves may not mean a lot to the reader, but an indication of their significance is that the overall literacy level rose 14 points between 1996 (when the survey first took place) and 2014. The gap between Pākehā and Māori is more than twice this.

Table 11.2: Adult Skills by Ethnicity, 2014 (Average Score)

	PĀKEHĀ	ASIAN	MĀORI	PASIFIKA
Literacy	287	267	254	242
Numeracy	280	264	247	223
Problem solving	292	278	277	261

Source: Ministry of Education, 2016

Even so, the average Māori literacy skill rose 20 points over the period, faster than the national total. Indeed, the Māori level in 2014 is only a little below the level of the total population in 1996. Again, Māori attainment is roughly a generation behind the Pākehā level.

(Numeracy levels were first measured in 2006. They suggest a not-dissimilar rate of gain for Māori over the shorter period, as for literacy (5 points against 7 points); 2014 was the first time problem solving was included in the survey.)

Another way of judging the data is to compare the scores with other countries. In literacy skills, New Zealand was fourth out of 29 OECD countries in 2014. If they had belonged to a separate country, Māori would have been 25th equal. In numeracy skills, New Zealand was 13th; Māori would have been 26th equal. In problem-solving skills, New Zealand was fifth; Māori would have been 22nd equal.[62]

These scores apply to the whole of the adult population, so

comparisons do not allow for different age structures. Because the Māori population is younger, and because the skills tend to be higher among younger adults, an age-adjusted companion would show an even greater gap between Māori and Pākehā. (Gender specific scores are not available.)

The data by distribution of scores is not available. The 1996 survey found '[t]he majority of Māori, Pacific Islands people and those from other ethnic minority groups are functioning below the level of competence in literacy required to effectively meet the demands of everyday life'. There are scattered indications that the proportions of those with low literacy have been declining since then.

Immediately following this 'key finding' is the reminder that 'labour force status and income are related to level of literacy'.

Educational Attainment of Fifteen Year-olds

Every three years, the OECD surveys the attainments of 15 year-olds in reading (since 2000), mathematics (since 2003) and science literacy (since 2006). The 2012 scores are shown in Table 11.3.

Table 11.3: Educational Attainment by Ethnicity, 2012 (PISA Reading Literacy Mean Scores)

	TOTAL	MĀORI
Reading	512	466
Mathematics	500	452
Science	516	469

Source: Ministry of Education, 2015

Once again, Māori (and Pasifika) average levels on all three dimensions are substantially below the total (and even further below Pākehā levels, since the total includes Māori and Pasifika).

Another way of looking at the data is the proportion of the population in the bottom two of five attainment levels. Those in that proportion lack the competencies that will enable them to participate effectively in ordinary life situations. For each dimension, just over a quarter of Māori were down there; in contrast, the proportion for students as a whole was below a sixth.

Comparing the scores with other cities/countries participating in the 2012 survey, New Zealand is 13th out of 65 on reading skills, 23rd on mathematical skills and 18th on science knowledge skills. Had they belonged to a separate country, Māori would have been 41st on all three dimensions.

The author (Easton 2013) examined the raw scores of the PISA 2012 exercise by ethnicity and gender, looking only at Māori who described themselves as sole-Māori or Māori-Pākehā. (Sole-Māori were 44% of all Māori, Māori-Pākehā were 40%, and 16% described themselves as Māori and some other ethnicity. The latter group is not reported here.)

The scores for reading, mathematics and science literacy are reported in Table 11.4. Scores exceeding the OECD average are shown in bold.

In all dimensions Pākehā are well above the OECD averages, as are the national averages, by the equivalent of at least a year of schooling. (See Table 11.5.)

The scores for sole-Māori are about a year of schooling behind the OECD average, but the scores of the group that describes itself as both Māori and Pākehā are comfortably above the OECD average, although not as spectacularly as for sole-Pākehā. When the sole-Māori and Māori-Pākehā groups are pooled their averages are below the OECD, although much closer than in the case for sole-Māori.

Socioeconomic Status

It is well established that educational achievement is related to socioeconomic status (SES), while there is a correlation between SES and ethnicity. When this is allowed for, there is a distinct rising (and statistically significant) trend from the score in lower to higher SES deciles. (However, the Māori and Māori-Pākehā scores are below the Pākehā ones in each socioeconomic decile; even so, those of the combined Māori groups in the top third of the socioeconomic ranking are higher than Pākehā at the bottom third of the ranking.)

The gradients are summarised in Table 11.5. The measure shown is the estimate of the difference between the average score at the bottom decile and the top gradient.

Table 11.4: Mean PISA Scores by Ethnicity and Gender

	BOYS	GIRLS	TOTAL
READING			
Pākehā	528	566	547
Māori	440	474	457
Māori-Pākehā	488	538	513
Both	461	507	484
TOTAL NZ	503	543	524
OECD	474	513	493
MATHEMATICS			
Pākehā	550	537	544
Māori	462	450	455
Māori-Pākehā	511	505	508
Both*	483	478	481
TOTAL NZ	528	516	521
OECD	501	490	496
SCIENCE LITERACY			
Pākehā	563	560	562
Māori	466	465	466
Māori-Pākehā	514	529	522
Both*	487	498	493
TOTAL NZ	534	535	535
OECD	501	499	501

Source: Easton (2013)

* Combined sole-Māori and Māori-Pākehā numbers.

Table 11.5: Difference in Educational Achievement Between Top and Bottom SES Decile

AVERAGE SCORE DIFFERENCE	READING		MATHEMATICS		SCIENCE LITERACY	
	BOYS	GIRLS	BOYS	GIRLS	BOYS	GIRLS
Pākehā	105	102	92	112	100	97
Māori	45	92	46	78	53	109
Māori-Pākehā	117	106	109	143	124	123
Both*	87	112	84	132	95	128
1 Year**	44		50		43	

Source: Easton (2013)
* Combined sole-Māori and Māori-Pākehā numbers.
** OECD estimate of the effect of one school year.

Typically students from the highest SES families average more than two years ahead in their achievement relative to those in the bottom SES families. However, the gradients for sole Māori boys are lower — only about a year — (less so for girls). Gradients of Māori-Pākehā exceed the Pākehā ones; there is a convergence of attainment with rising socioeconomic status. That also applies to Māori girls when the two ethnic groups are pooled. The higher gradients that the gap between these ethnicity achievement scores is proportionally greater at the low SES level than at the high level.[63]

It would appear a bottom SES family requires two extra years of schooling to catch up to a top SES family. In practice, students in the low SES families are likely to get fewer, rather than more, years of schooling.

This effect of ethnic groups not being spread evenly through the SES ranking can be eliminated by deriving an average as if the two groups had exactly the same socioeconomic structure. When the adjustment (i.e. control for SES) is made, the scores for the Both group (i.e. combined sole-Māori and Māori-Pākehā group) prove to be close to the OECD average, and are as good as or slightly better than students in Britain and the US.

These results apply for 15-year-olds in 2012. In principle, other years could be rather different. But in practice, the gap between Māori and Pākehā, the difference between Māori and Māori-Pākehā, and the significance of socioeconomic status is likely to have persisted through the years.

(It would be remiss not to mention the conclusions that New Zealand's average scores on each of the three subjects has declined since 2009 (and earlier), and that the performance has also declined relative to other countries. That is also true for Māori.)

Conclusion

At the age of 15, Māori students are on average educationally behind Pākehā; about a quarter of them have not reached educational levels that give them competence to function well in society. Not surprisingly, this weakness is transmitted into low skills when they are adults, and they have fewer (or lower) qualifications. The consequence is that on average Māori have inferior employment opportunities and lower incomes compared to Pākehā.

Careful analysis rejects that there is a significant inherent genetic or cultural reason for this poor average performance. As argued, it reflects Māori history when, some generations back, they came from a rural context where urban skills were not in such great demand and where they received schooling of a lower quality than Pākehā.

The patterns have continued over the generations through a dynamic process in which the families (and extended families) play a crucial role.[64] Families whose adults have poor educational attainment are unlikely to pass on the foundational skills required to enable their children to make the best possible use of their talents, nor to engender the attitudes and experiences that enable them to seize available opportunities — especially those facilitated by the education system.

Consequently, the education system is not as effective for children from such backgrounds and they end up with the poor scores reported by the PISA survey, and the poor adult competencies identified by the PIAAC survey. Inevitably, those on this track are likely to end up with inferior qualifications (if any), employment opportunities and income.

Too often their children will go through the same circle of lost educational opportunity; a repeated cycle reinforced by the family instability that tends to go with these educational and economic characteristics.

This does not happen to all children brought up in family circumstances of educational disadvantage. Some succeed through luck or exceptional ability, but the evidence concludes that the majority do not. Arguably, there is a very slow convergence — an uplifting of attainment at the bottom — despite far-from-comprehensive efforts at preschool, school, tertiary educational institutions and adult literacy programmes. Sufficient attention is not paid to the dynamic process, nor to the family's role in the cycle.

Bibliography

Easton, B. (2013), *Ethnicity, Gender, Socioeconomic Status and Educational Achievement: An Exploration.* PPTA, Wellington.

Ministry of Education (2015), *PISA 2012: New Zealand Summary Report.* Ministry of Education, Wellington.

Ministry of Education (2016), *Skills in New Zealand and Around the Word.* Ministry of Education, Wellington.

Statistics New Zealand (various years), *NZ Stats.* Statistics NZ, Wellington.

CHAPTER 12 | EMPLOYMENT

Paid employment is important because it is the main source of income, but it also has latent functions, including giving social status and involving the individual in the community in a structured way.

Unfortunately the data in this area is limited. The numbers in the Household Labour Force Survey are too small to trace changes in smaller social groups; the Population Census, used here, is comprehensive but what is published is not available at a sufficiently disaggregated level to do anything more than pose questions.

The Employment Participation Rate

It is common to compare unemployment rates by ethnicity. However, they do not cover those who have become so discouraged after unsuccessfully looking for work that they cease to be actively seeking employment. In such cases, they are no longer defined as unemployed in the standard definition.

Instead of the unemployment rate, here we use the employment participation rate: the proportion of those in the working-age group (16–65) who are in employment. It, in effect, measures all those who are not employed, whether they are actively seeking work or not.

The measure is becoming increasingly popular among economists because it is less sensitive to the definition of unemployment. On the other hand, the standard definition of employment is that the individual is working for at least one hour per week in the paid workforce, although the worker may want more work (he or she is 'underemployed').

This is a problem encountered with conventional unemployment rate measures too. Note that some of those not employed may be involved with unpaid voluntary work or may be working in the unpaid, non-market economy — say, caring for children or doing housework.[65]

There are two major caveats. First, the standard employment measure ignores that those in full-time education and training may not be 'employed'; yet it seems wrong to treat them as simply not in the workforce, and it can lead to odd results.[66] The second caveat arises because we know different ethnicities have different fertility patterns — especially by age — which may lead to different employment and non-employment patterns by age because of different times focusing on full-time childcare. In principle adjustments can be made for such phenomena, but the data is not readily available at the moment.

Because of the different age structures of the various ethnic groups, it would be best to compare the employment rates by cohort.

Table 12.1: Employment Participation Rates by Age and Ethnicity (Percentage)

AGE GROUP	ALL	MĀORI
15–19 years	33.7	29.7
20–24 years	65.0	55.8
25–29 years	73.6	59.1
30–34 years	75.2	63.6
35–39 years	77.3	67.8
40–44 years	80.2	70.0
45–49 years	81.7	70.7
50–54 years	81.1	70.7
55–59 years	77.4	67.5
60–64 years	67.8	61.2
65 years and over	22.1	26.2
TOTAL	62.3	56.5

Source: Statistics New Zealand, 2013 Population Census

Table 12.1 shows the employment rate by age group in the 2013 Population Census.[67] (Unfortunately there is no data by gender and age.) The table shows the employment rate for Māori is almost always lower than for all. In total it is about 10% lower.[68] This is probably a truer measure of the difference in relative unemployment rates between Māori and the population as a whole. The census reported rates were 10.4% for Māori and 4.8% for all, a difference of 5.6 percentage points. That is because the unemployment rate measure does not allow for discouraged unemployed. The implication is that Māori start off with an income deficit relative to the population at large, even before allowing for different earnings rates and hours worked, simply because they are less likely to be in the paid labour force.

There are differences between ages. The low participation rates among the young reflect that many are in full-time education. The relatively low participation rates for Māori in their twenties in part reflects that Māori women are having children and not in the paid workforce. But when non-Māori have their children at a later age, they have better paid opportunities and return to the paid labour force earlier, perhaps using paid (possibly subsidised) early childhood education. The higher participation rate for Māori over 65 years old probably arises because they have lower levels of occupational superannuation and retirement savings. A higher incidence of sickness and disability also reduces Māori employment participation.

Table 12.2 gives the average employment participation rates by ethnicity and gender. The female participation rates are just over 10 percentage points below the male ones for all ethnicities. The ethnic differences are much the same as in Table 12.1. Intriguingly, those who classify themselves as Māori–Pākehā have employment

Table 12.2: Employment Participation Rates by Ethnicity and Gender (Percentage)

	FEMALE	MALE
Pākehā	64.0	75.1
Māori–Pākehā	65.7	75.8
Sole-Māori	57.9	69.7

Source: Household Labour Force Survey, average 2007Q4–2016Q2

responses similar to Pākehā — not halfway between. They may be slightly higher because of different age profiles. The database does not allow us to explore this.

Occupations

The differences in patterns of occupations by ethnicity are hardly surprising given the differences in education and qualifications. Table 12.3 shows the proportions of Māori in the main occupational groups reported in the 2006 and 2013 censuses.

Māori make up 11% of the workforce as a whole, but are higher in the categories for relatively unskilled occupations and, broadly, less represented in skilled occupations. (Sales workers are puzzling because most supermarket workers would not be considered 'skilled'.) The same pattern would be evident within each occupational category; there would be relatively more Māori in the least-skilled part of it.

The cheerful news is that the imbalance generally converged between 2006 and 2013.[69] While the proportion of Māori in the workforce remained the same at 11%, there tended to be reductions in the proportion of Māori in the least-skilled and increases in the more-skilled occupations.

Table 12.3: Percentage of Māori Employed in Each Occupational Category

OCCUPATION	2006	2013
Labourers	20.0	19.2
Machinery operators & drivers	18.9	17.9
Community & personal service workers	14.5	14.4
TOTAL	**11.0**	**11.0**
Technicians & trades workers	10.6	10.3
Sales workers	9.5	9.8
Clerical & administrative workers	9.3	9.7
Professionals	7.7	8.0
Managers	7.0	7.7

Source: Statistics New Zealand, Population Censuses

Industries

The differences in the patterns of employment by industry show less marked divergences than that for occupation (see Table 12.4).

Interestingly, despite a widespread perception, Māori participation in accommodation and food services (including tourism) and the primary sector (agriculture, forestry and fishing) is not particularly

Table 12.4: Percentage of Māori Employed Each Industry Sector

INDUSTRY SECTOR	2006	2013
Transport, postal & warehousing	15.0	14.0
Electricity, gas, water & waste services	15.2	14.0
Mining	17.3	13.9
Manufacturing	13.9	13.7
Public administration & safety	13.6	13.6
Administrative & support services	12.3	12.7
Construction	13.3	12.6
Education & training	11.7	12.3
Arts & recreation services	11.5	12.3
Accommodation & food services	12.7	11.9
Agriculture, forestry & fishing	11.5	11.8
Health care & social assistance	11.0	11.0
TOTAL	**11.0**	**11.0**
Other services	9.9	10.1
Retail trade	9.5	9.7
Information media & telecommunications	8.4	8.5
Wholesale trade	8.1	7.9
Rental, hiring & real estate services	8.3	7.7
Financial & insurance services	6.6	7.1
Professional, scientific & technical services	5.9	5.9

Source: Statistics New Zealand, Population Censuses

high, although slightly above average. They are particularly involved in transport, postal and warehousing; electricity, gas, water and waste services; and mining.[70]

Māori are exceptionally underrepresented in the highly qualified, well-paid and expanding financial and insurance services/professional, scientific and technical services sectors, although there was a rapid expansion of Māori participation in the former between 2006 and 2013.

Conclusion

In one sense this chapter does not tell us much that is not generally known, although it provides important caveats. It suggests unemployment is effectively much higher among Māori than generally realised if those that feel discouraged from seeking work are included. It confirms Māori tend to be in low-skilled occupations, although there appears to have been some relative upgrading over time. It also confirms Māori tend to work more in the primary sector and tourism, but not as much as is generally thought, and that there are other industrial sectors where Māori are more intensively employed.

Even so, the analysis has been riddled by hypotheses: including that gender and childcare patterns are important, that there is a need for more care with those in full-time education when considering young adults, and that elderly Māori have different behaviours relative to the population at large.

Given that further data exists and can be used to explore these hypotheses — notably hours worked, employment status[71] and voluntary work — and in some areas it is possible to make comparisons over time or at a finer level, there seems a strong case for a major study on Māori employment using available data that can be unlocked, albeit with effort and resources.

Yet strangely, reports on the 'Māori Economy' are thin on details of Māori employment, even though it is the most important dimension in the Māori economy.

Bibliography

Statistics New Zealand (various years), *Household Labour Force Survey*. Statistics NZ, Wellington.

Statistics New Zealand (2006 and 2013), *Population Census*. Statistics NZ, Wellington.

CHAPTER 13 | HEALTH

Systematic comparative ethnic health studies are bedevilled by the requirement of getting consistent definitions. The Health Inequalities Research Programme (HIRP), hosted by the University of Otago, Wellington, found the ethnicity appearing on a death certificate is not always the ethnicity people report in the Census. Since the former is the basis for the numerator of a mortality ratio and the latter the denominator, they had to adjust the data to ensure consistency.[72] (Blakely *et al* 2002) The result is an extremely useful research programme, some of which is reported below.

The focus is on life expectation at birth, which combines the individual mortality ratios in each age group into a single indicator.[73]

However, the results suffer from the limitation that the mortality and the resulting life expectancy it reports are not comprehensive measures of health. Increasingly, health care is concerned with improving the quality of a person's life as well as extending it. At present, the nearest we can get to a population-wide quality-of-life measure is the 'independent life expectancy' reported below.

Life Expectation

Table 13.1 shows the life expectations in 1946 and 2006 for Māori and non-Māori by gender. Life expectancy has been increasing. Over 65 years, it increased by 13 years for non-Māori. (That means that if born a year later, one is likely to live an extra 10 weeks.) Non-Māori enjoy a considerable advantage over Māori. In 2011, it was 6–7 years. (A way of thinking about this is that Māori life expectancy in 2011 was the same as that of non-Māori about 25 years earlier.)

Table 13.1: Life Expectation by Ethnicity by Gender, 1946–2006 (years)

YEAR	MĀORI		NON-MĀORI	
	FEMALE	MALE	FEMALE	MALE
1946	48	49	70	67
2011	77	73	83	80
Difference	29	24	13	13

Source: T. Blakely (pers. comm.) but see Woodward and Blakely (2015, Figure 7)

However, in 1946 Māori life expectancy was around 20 years behind the non-Māori level. There was a strong improvement in Māori life expectancy in the two decades after World War II, attributed to rapid falls in infant mortality, respiratory diseases and TB. The improvement was so rapid that it offset the harms from evolving chronic diseases, especially heart disease. Māori life expectancy was catching up to the non-Māori level.

It is not shown here, but in the data Māori progress levelled off in the 1980s and 1990s. This is not evident in the non-Māori data, although there were long periods of stagnation associated with the peaking of the ischemic heart disease epidemic.

The exact reasons for the Māori stagnation are not known, but they do coincide with a weakening labour market from the late 1980s and the health redisorganisation of the early 1990s. Additionally, the impact of the heart disease had different timings for Māori and non-Māori.

Since 1996 there have been steady improvements for both Māori and non-Māori, together with some catch-up by Māori.

Table 13.2 shows the percentage contribution of various conditions to the difference between Māori and non-Māori mortality rates. There is not much difference between the two columns by gender, while the main causes of differences in mortality are also the main causes of mortality for all ethnicities, indicating the Māori 'problem' is across the board.

Table 13.2: Percentage Contribution of Each Condition to the Māori: European/Other Absolute Gap in Cause-specific Mortality Rates, Aged 1–74 Years, By Sex, 1981–2004

CAUSE OF DEATH	FEMALES	MALES
Cardiovascular disease	42.0%	42.6%
All cancer	23.0%	20.0%
Chronic lung disease	10.2%	6.0%
Unintentional injury	3.4%	8.6%
Suicide	- 0.4%	0.6%
Other causes	21.8%	21.2%

Source: Tobias et. al., Table 1

Independent Life Expectancy

A study combined results from the 2013 Disability Survey and the 2012–14 period life tables to calculate the expected years of independent life.[74] This is a step towards measuring quality of life. Key results are shown in Table 13.3.

Table 13.3: Average Years of Life Expectancy At Birth, 2013

STATUS	MĀORI		NON-MĀORI	
	FEMALE	MALE	FEMALE	MALE
Independent life expectancy	60.4	54.3	67.4	66.7
Life expectancy with dependency	16.7	18.7	16.5	13.6
Total life expectancy	77.1	73.0	83.9	80.3

Source: Ministry of Health (2015)

While non-Māori females born in 2013 were expected to live an average of 83.9 years, some 16.5 of these years are lived with at least one disability for which they need support. The comparable figures for non-Māori males are 80.3 and 13.6 years.

A Māori female is expected to live 77.1 years, of which 16.7 years will be with a disability for which they need support. They live almost seven years less than non-Māori females, but during their lifetime they have much the same number of years restricted by disability. Māori males are expected to live 73 years, but 18.7 years will be with disability. This contrasts with 80.3 years for non-Māori males, who suffer only 13.6 years of dependency (less than females because they do not live as long). While the difference in life expectancy between Māori and non-Māori is thought to be about seven years, the difference in years of independent life for males is more than 12 years; for females, it is seven years.

The results of disability surveys and period life tables back to 1996 suggest people are living longer but spending more time in dependent health states. Apart from Māori males, the independent life expectancy at birth increased by 0.5–2.2 years for all groups between 1996 and 2013. However, Māori male independent life expectancy decreased from 56 years in 1996 to 54.3 years in 2013; the gain in life expectancy has been in low-quality years, with some loss in years of independent life.[75]

These results suggest Māori are likely, on average, to have a poorer quality of life than others — as well as shorter lives.

Social Effects

There is some evidence that some social characteristics affect longevity by ethnicity. Table 13.4 summarises the evidence of the impact of smoking on life expectancy.

Perhaps surprisingly, smoking appears to shorten Māori lives less than non-Māori ones. This may be because smoking is interacting

Table 13.4: Life Expectation in Years by Ethnicity and Smoking Status, 1996

STATUS	MĀORI		NON-MĀORI	
	FEMALE	MALE	FEMALE	MALE
Current smoker	69.5	63.8	76.0	70.9
Never smoked	73.4	68.1	82.2	78.5
Gain	3.9	4.3	6.2	7.6

Source: Carter et. al. (2010)

with other effects more closely associated with Māori, such as poor-quality housing and unemployment. Because more Māori smoke, in total Māori may proportionally make greater year gains than non-Māori by stopping smoking. Regardless, there are clearly gains to be made in longevity, and almost certainly quality of life, through all New Zealanders not smoking.

Table 13.5 summarises the impact of income (measured by census) on life expectancy.[76]
Māori gain about a year over non-Māori by shifting from low incomes to high incomes. Again, there may be other associated effects cutting

Table 13.5: Life Expectation by Ethnicity and Income, 2001

STATUS	MĀORI		NON-MĀORI	
	FEMALE	MALE	FEMALE	MALE
Lower income	71.3	65.6	79.8	74.0
Medium income	73.9	69.5	81.6	76.8
Higher income	76.6	72.5	83.9	79.7
High-low difference	5.3	6.9	4.1	5.7

Source: Carter et. al. (2010)

across this result. But insofar as it is robust, it implies Māori health tends to be more damaged by an increase in income inequality, given they are proportionally poorer at the bottom of the income distribution.[77]

Conclusion

As measured by mortality and independent life expectancy, Māori have poorer health. They live fewer years and have poorer-quality health during those years. While there has been some catch-up in the post-war era, there has been relative stagnation in recent years, and in the case of Māori men some evidence of retrogression.

These tabulations do not allow for the impact of other effects that may interact with the reported variables. For instance, low income tends to be associated with low-quality housing, which also influences health. Unemployment is bad for health and for incomes.

A particular issue is whether there are in fact no specific Māori health problems; their poor health could be a consequence of social factors Māori are more likely to experience. The HIRP results reported here do not provid a definitive conclusion — inevitably, given the coverage of the census questions and (probably) the size of the samples.[78] But they incline to the conclusion that social factors of all kinds play a major part in determining poorer Māori health.

What is unchallengeable is that Māori life expectations are markedly lower than those of non-Māori (more specifically Pākehā, since Pasifika are similar to Māori in this case). It is unlikely this is mainly a 'genetic' effect, given most Māori also have non-Māori ancestors. Probably much more important are the life circumstances of Māori, perhaps compounded by institutions being insensitive to particular Māori behaviour.[79]

Bibliography

Blakely, T.A., B. Robson, J. Atkinson, J., et. al. (2002), 'Unlocking the Numerator-denominator Bias. I: Adjustments Ratios by Ethnicity for 1991–94 Mortality Data. The New Zealand Census Mortality Study.' *NZ Medical Journal* 2002; Vol. 115, No. 1147, pp. 39–43.

Blakely, T. (2011), 'Health Equity and Social Determinants of Health'. Presentation to The Marmot Symposium. Wellington School of Medicine, Wellington.

Carter, K., T. Blakely and M. Soeberg (2001), 'Trends in survival and life expectancy by ethnicity, income and smoking in New Zealand: 1980s to 2000s.' *NZ Medical Journal* 2010; Vol. 115, No. 1320, pp. 13–24.

Woodward, A. and T. Blakely (2014), *The Healthy Country? A History of Life and Death in New Zealand.* AUP, Auckland.

Tobias, M., T. Blakely, D. Matheson, K. Rasanathan and J. Atkinson. J. (2009), 'Changing trends in indigenous inequalities in mortality: lessons from New Zealand'. *International Journal of Epidemiology* 2009; Vol. 38, No. 6, pp. 1711–22.

Ministry of Health (2015), *Independent Life Expectancy in New Zealand 2013.* Ministry of Health, Wellington.

This chapter has benefited from Tony Blakely reviewing an earlier draft.

CHAPTER 14 | INCOMES

As elsewhere, it is possible the ethnic definitions are not consistent throughout this data. Unfortunately, it is not possible to standardise as was done in the chapter on health.

The concept of income also presents a difficulty. This chapter uses 'market incomes', 'gross income' (market incomes plus benefits) and 'disposable income' (gross incomes less income taxes). The unit may be 'personal' (typically only adults) or 'households', in which the household income is spread though all its members, including children. (Chapter 9 covers wealth.)

Personal Earnings

The New Zealand Income Survey (NZIS) is run each year during the June quarter as a supplement to the Household Labour Force Survey. The earnings for Māori in paid employment relative to Pākehā are shown in Table 14.1.

This compares Māori against Pākehā, partly to avoid double counting (since Māori are a part of all) but also to eliminate Pasifika (who, like Māori, are below average, perhaps for similar reasons) and Asians (which include a big group of university students and also some very wealthy immigrants).

The median (middle of the distribution) relativity is higher than the average, or mean.[80] That will be because Māori are more bunched at the bottom of the distribution, while conversely Pākehā are spread towards the top.

The ratio of the means to medians gives a measure of the relative inequality of the two distributions. The ratios in Table 14.1 indicate

Māori earnings are more equally distributed than Pākehā, and they are more equally distributed for Māori men relative to Pākehā men, than for Māori women relative to Pākehā women. (An alternative way of putting it is that the Māori woman distribution is more like the Pākehā one than the Māori men's is like the Pākehā men's.)

Table 14.1: Earnings for Māori in Paid Employment Relative to Pākehā[81], Average for 1998–2015, Ages 25–64[89]

	AVERAGE	MEDIAN	RATIO
Female	86.9%	91.1%	97.4%
Male	79.3%	83.3%	95.1%

Source: New Zealand Income Survey

However, the Māori male relativity (to Pākehā men) is considerably lower than the Māori female relativity (to Pākehā females): 79% for the male mean versus 87% for the female mean, and 83% for the male median versus 91% for the female median.

Of course, male earnings are higher than female earnings. In the case of Māori, average female earnings are about 74% of average male earnings — the median relativity for Māori is about 77%. The Pākehā female ones are about 66% for means (and 71% for medians). The percentage weekly difference is greater than for hourly rates because women work fewer paid hours than men.

The data confirms the unsurprising conclusion that Māori earnings are lower than Pākehā earnings. The surprising conclusion is, perhaps, that this is more strongly a male effect.

Table 14.1 gives only the averages for the survey's 18-year period. This is because a statistical exploration shows that while there is considerable year-to-year variation — almost certainly reflecting sampling error, but also perhaps the business cycle — there is no statistically significant trend. The underlying level in 1998 was much the same as it was in 2015.

Personal Incomes

Table 14.2 shows the before-tax personal incomes (including earnings, investment income and social security transfers) for Māori and non-Māori from the NZIS. There is not a more detailed ethnic breakdown, nor one by gender.

Again we find adult Māori incomes are lower than those of non-Māori: a fifth by average, a sixth by median. Again, the non-Māori income distribution is more unequal than the Māori one. Again, only the average over the period need be shown because there is no statistical trend.[83]

Table 14.2: All Māori Incomes Relative to Non-Māori, Average for 1998–2015, 25–64 years[84]

	AVERAGE	MEDIAN	RATIO
All Māori	79.1%	84.2%	93.9%

Source: New Zealand Income Survey

Table 14.3 gives some indication of the composition of the total (before-tax) income of Māori and non-Māori adults aged over 15 by source. While both are dependent primarily upon wages and salaries, non-Māori get more than twice the proportion from self-employment and four times the proportion from investment incomes. On the other hand, Māori incomes are more dependent upon government transfers, in part because their earnings are close to benefit levels.[85]

Table 14.3: Sources of Before-tax Income by Ethnicity, 2002–2015

	MĀORI	NON-MĀORI
Wage & salary	71.5%	66.2%
Self-employed	7.1%	15.7%
Government transfers	20.2%	12.0%
Investment income	1.5%	6.1%
Total	100%	100%

Source: New Zealand Income Survey

Census Incomes

The NZI sample is not large enough to examine the distributional differences between Māori and the population as a whole. The Census covers the whole population, although it is likely the income recall of census respondents is less accurate than for the NZIS. It is possible to go back to the 1981 Census: earlier ones used a different definition of income.[86] The ethnicity characterisations may differ over time.

Subject to these caveats, Table 14.4 shows the distributional differences for seven censuses between the total incomes (before tax and including government transfers) between Māori and the entire adult population as follows. The total population is divided into five income quintiles with the proportion of Māori in each of those quintiles shown. Thus in the 2013 census, only 11.9% of Māori adults were in the top income quintile, in comparison with 20% of the whole population. At the other end, 26.2% of Māori were in the bottom quintile in contrast to 20% of the whole population.

Table 14.4: Percent of Māori in Each Total Adult Population Quintile

	TOP	SECOND	MIDDLE	FOURTH	BOTTOM
1981	11.0%	20.7%	19.3%	18.9%	30.1%
1986	11.6%	20.6%	23.1%	20.7%	24.0%
1991	10.2%	17.7%	22.2%	26.1%	23.9%
1996	11.8%	18.9%	21.3%	23.1%	24.9%
2001	11.4%	19.4%	22.0%	22.4%	24.7%
2006	12.0%	20.0%	23.2%	21.3%	23.7%
2013	11.9%	19.1%	21.0%	21.9%	26.2%

Source: New Zealand Population censuses

The basic conclusion is that throughout the 30-odd years, Māori are more likely to be at the bottom of the income distribution, and are relatively rare at the top.

Although one might discern a trend of a rising proportion in the bottom and the top quintiles (after omitting the 1981 observation), the change is not statistically significant. Were it significant, it might imply increasing inequality among Māori incomes. The mean-to-median ratio broadly confirms the pattern of increasing Māori inequality relative to all incomes, but again the change is not statistically significant.

Household Incomes

The household income variable is derived by a number of transformations from the personal incomes used earlier in the chapter. First, income taxes have been deducted from total (gross) personal income (including government transfers), which gives 'disposable income'. The disposable income of the individuals in each household is then aggregated into 'total household disposable income'. Total household income is then divided among the inhabitants, including children, to give 'equivalised household (disposable) income'.[87] It is recorded by individuals, so a five-person household appears five times.

Once again the Household Survey sample size is not large and such statistics as there are tend to be coarse and fragmentary, making it difficult to explore the Māori household income distribution in any detail.

Household Incomes in New Zealand combines the three survey years 2011–2013 to estimate the proportions of children (aged 0–17) below the poverty line, finding 34% of Māori are in this category compared to 17% of Pākehā (and 23% of all children).[88] Even so, Māori children make up 34% of the total poor compared to 38% who are Pākehā — despite Pākehā being a much more numerous ethnic group. (Perry 2017: Table H8)

The result can be cross checked with an independent hardship measure. Some 39% of Māori children are on the lowest hardship level (a score of six hardship characteristics or more) and 11% on the highest level (11 or more). In contrast, the proportions for Pākehā are 18% and 5% respectively. (Perry 2017: Table D9)

The longitudinal Survey of Family Income and Employment (SOFIE) enables an assessment of the persistence of the state of poverty. On average, 36% of the Māori population (including adults) were below the poverty line in 'current poverty'. However, 32% were in 'chronic poverty', that is, on average below the poverty line for all seven years, or 'waves'.[89] (Perry 2017: Table K9) In contrast, only 15% of the entire population were in current poverty and 11% were in chronic poverty.[90]

In summary, relative to Pākehā, poverty rates are high among Māori — especially parents/guardians and their children — and they are persistent. (A comprehensive account would draw attention to Pasifika poverty and hardship rates being similar to the Māori ones.)

There is one available data series that enables some assessment of household income trends over time. Table 14.5 shows the ratio of Māori to Pākehā median household incomes from 1988 to 2015.[91]

Table 14.5: Maori Median (Equivalised) Household Income Relative to Pākehā:1988–2016

YEAR	RATIO
1988	82.9
1990	75.1
1992	68.1
1994	69.8
1996	79.8
1998	77.3

YEAR	RATIO
2001	81.2
2004	74.6
2007	73.8
2008	78.6
2009	75.8
2010	77.1

YEAR	RATIO
2011	69.9
2012	80.6
2013	74.1
2014	70.7
2015	72.0
2016	78.7

Source: Perry (2017: Table D5)

Unfortunately we have only one observation before neoliberal redistribution policies began to be introduced in the late 1980s. Compared to the later observations, the 1988 statistic suggests the Māori-to-All (adjusted) income ratio was higher then, at 83%, than after the redistributional measures (mainly in 1989 to 1991).

In the early 1990s the ratio fell dramatically, implying Māori were more heavily affected by the redistributional policies, together with the very high rates of unemployment at the time. (Easton 1995)

When unemployment returned to more 'normal' levels, the ratio recovered to an average of 76% in the 1996–2016 period.[92] However, the average over the period may be misleading. Statistically, there is no significant trend over the period. Māori household incomes have not been catching up with Pākehā ones. The change is a consequence of the addition of the 2016 year. That one observation can do this says be cautious when interpreting the data.

(There is an upward tick in the level for the year to June 2016, the last available observation. The shift is within the variation from sampling error over the period. There may be some effect from the increase in benefit rates (above inflation) of $25 per family with children, from April 2016, although this occurred only for three months of the 2016 year.)

Conclusion

Māori incomes are lower than Pākehā incomes. Their earnings are lower, with Māori male earnings being relatively lower than Māori female ones. They have less investment income, while government transfers such as social security do not offset the overall deficit.

There is no evidence of a recent trend in the relativities of market incomes. Māori market incomes are below Pākehā ones, but the evidence is that over the last two decades — as far back as we can go — the gap is neither increasing nor decreasing.

The pattern of (equivalised) household (disposable) incomes is a little more complex. The neoliberal redistributional policies at the end of the 1980s and early 1990s may have dropped the relativity from 83% to an average 76% (after even more depressed levels of the high unemployment era of the early 1990s). Since then there has been no evident trend in the relativity. Māori household incomes are behind and they are not catching up.

To conclude on a personal note: I have been monitoring trends in Māori incomes for about 40 years. My conclusion, at first and for some decades, was that there was a very slow convergence of Māori incomes towards non-Māori ones. This report, using much finer data than I had then, suggests that either I was wrong (perhaps pushing the data more than was justified) or that the convergence has ceased. The explanation for the latter might be that the urbanisation of Māori increased their market incomes, but that shift is now over and relative stagnation has followed. Even so, I am surprised that there has not been some subsequent convergence. One might expect it for a subgroup in a market, even if overall inequality was not reducing. It is almost as if (many) Māori are trapped at the bottom of the economy. Part I explains why that might be so.

Bibliography

Easton, B. (1995), 'Poverty in New Zealand — 1981 to 1993', *New Zealand Sociology,* November 1995, Vol. 10, No. 2, pp. 182–214.

Easton, B. (2013), 'Economic Inequality in New Zealand: a User's Guide', *The New Zealand Journal of Sociology,* Vol. 28, Issue 3, pp. 9–66.

Perry, B. (2017), *Household Incomes in New Zealand: Trends in Indicators of Inequality and Hardship: 1982 to 2016.* MSD, Wellington.

Statistics New Zealand (various years), *New Zealand Income Survey.* Statistics NZ, Wellington.

Statistics New Zealand (various years), *Population Census.* Statistics NZ, Wellington.

CHAPTER 15

THE CRIMINAL JUSTICE SYSTEM

This chapter depends heavily upon a 2007 Department of Corrections Report, *Over-representation of Māori in the Criminal Justice System: An Exploratory Report*.[93] While the report is over a decade old (its statistics could benefit from being updated, and there has been subsequent research), its analytic conclusions remain robust.

While the report is about New Zealand Māori (though other ethnicities are also covered for some purposes), it is part of an international research programme applied to New Zealand. To some extent then, its conclusions are not so much about Māori as about universal social processes illustrated by Māori in New Zealand.

The report has the now-mandatory warnings of the difficulties of defining Māori, the different ethnic age profiles — criminal activity tends to be most intense among young adults — and problems with the statistics.

The Over-representation of Māori in the Criminal Justice System

The report summarises the over-representation of Māori in the criminal justice system as follows (the specific numbers refer to about 2007, when the report was written):

> Relative to their numbers in the general population, Māori are over-represented at every stage of the criminal justice process. Though forming just 12.5% of the general population aged 15 and over, 42% of all criminal

THE CRIMINAL JUSTICE SYSTEM | 113

apprehensions involve a person identifying as Māori, as do 50% of all persons in prison. For Māori women, the picture is even more acute: they comprise around 60% of the female prison population.

The true scale of Māori over-representation is greater than a superficial reading of such figures tends to convey. For example, with respect to the prison population, the rate of imprisonment for this country's non-Māori population is around 100 per 100,000. If that rate applied to Māori also, the number of Māori in prison at any one time would be no more than 650. There are, however, currently 4000 Māori in prison — six times the number one might otherwise expect.

Further, a recent extraction of court criminal history data indicated that over 16,000 Māori males currently between the ages of 20 and 29 years have a record of serving one or more sentences administered by the Department of Corrections. This equates to more than 30% of all Māori males in that age band; the corresponding figure for non-Māori appears to be around 10%. At any given point in time throughout the last decade, fully 3% of all Māori males between the ages of 20 and 29 years were in prison, either on remand or as sentenced prisoners; again, the corresponding figure for non-Māori is less than one sixth of that.

Over-representation in offender statistics is mirrored also by over-representation of Māori as victims of crime, a result of the fact that much crime occurs within families, social networks or immediate neighbourhoods.

Why Are Māori Over-represented?

The report describes two different explanatory approaches:

- that *bias* operates within the criminal justice system, such that any suspected or actual offending by Māori has harsher consequences for those Māori, resulting in an accumulation of individuals within the system; and

- that a range of *adverse early-life social and environmental factors* result in Māori being at greater risk of ending up in patterns of adult criminal conduct.

The two approaches are elaborated in the next two sections. The report concludes:

> [T]he two perspectives are by no means mutually exclusive, and both approaches appear to offer part of the explanation for the current state of affairs. The evidence points to an interaction between the two processes, where the operation of one set makes the other more likely. For example, early environmental influences may predispose individuals towards certain types of illegal or anti-social behaviour, which in turn raises the risk of police involvement. Additionally, the risk of apprehension is "amplified" because of formal and informal "profiling" by official agencies, as well as society generally.
>
> There are indications of a degree of over-representation related solely to ethnicity, rather than any other expected factor, at key points in the criminal justice system. Although mostly small at each point, the cumulative effect is likely to be sufficient to justify closer examination and investigation of options to reduce disproportionate representation of Māori.

The report's policy conclusion is that the primary domain for government intervention to address disproportionality resides in the areas of health, social support and education, in order to reduce disadvantage and the problems it confers. It says criminal justice-sector agencies could contribute to improving outcomes through early intervention strategies.

More is said in the chapter conclusion about the reinforcing cycles in the processes being described here.

Bias in the Justice System

A number of studies have shown a greater likelihood, associated only with ethnicity, for Māori offenders to:

have police contact;
be charged;

lack legal representation;
not be granted bail;
plead guilty;
be convicted;
be sentenced to non-monetary penalties; and
be denied release to home detention.

The report could not identify compelling evidence of bias at every step of the criminal justice decision-making process; much of the disparity is small and open to other possible explanations.

'Bias' may not be a good term for the phenomenon. The report suggests the difference 'often results not from deliberate discrimination, but from unconscious prejudice and stereotyping and as an unintended consequence of prima facie reasonable attitudes, practices, and decisions'.

Aggregate disproportionality of Māori in criminal justice statistics may, to some extent at least, be a cumulative effect, where the interactions of relatively small individual effects produce significant disparities in total at the national level. In other words, relatively minor biasing influences may combine to produce, at the end point, quite substantial effects.

Thus the report does not deny that ethnicity plays some small but tangible role at key decision-making points, in ways that are 'not intended by the justice system'. Many Māori would argue the bias is more significant than the Ministry report concludes. There would be a common agreement, though, that there is a need to monitor and reduce such bias.

The section of the report concludes, however, that it cannot realistically be suggested that current differences in the rate of imprisonment could arise solely from such bias effects.

Early-life Environmental Influences

The report goes on to argue that over the last three decades, international research has built up a wealth of knowledge to explain why some young people embark on a pathway that leads to persistent offending, while most do not, or do so only trivially.[94]

The childhood antecedents of chronic adult offending include the following key factors.

- Family structure, context and processes: examples include being born to young mothers, a lack of family stability, a family environment in which conflict and violence is common, and being exposed to harsh punishment.

- Individual characteristics of the developing child and adolescent: these include factors affecting the child's neurological development, and psychological temperament.

- Educational participation, engagement and achievement: this includes school absence, early leaving age and failure to achieve qualifications.

- The emergence of developmental disorders: included here are childhood conduct disorder, early onset of antisocial behaviour, and abuse of alcohol and other substances during adolescence.

Māori are disproportionately represented in each of the factors. The details and local research underpinning it are in the report. Given the international research, the case seems compelling that Māori over-representation in the criminal justice system rests on a foundation of early-life environmental influences, although these effects may be magnified by the biases identified in the previous section.

Conclusion

Māori are over-represented in the criminal justice system (including as victims of crimes). A Department of Corrections report identifies small biases operating within the criminal justice system, resulting in a greater number of individuals within the system; and a range of adverse early-life social and environmental factors putting Māori at greater risk of ending up in patterns of adult criminal conduct.

Why are Māori more prone to these early-life environmental influences than Pākehā? The answer lies in the historic paths of the two groups. Following an analysis of records of arrests and charges among Māori and Pacific people in Auckland (in 1966), L.S.W. Duncan concluded higher rates of offending resulted from the effect of migration (Māori from rural areas to urban, Pasifika from their island nations to New Zealand). He expected the differences would disappear in the next generation as 'assimilation' occurred. (Duncan 1972) They have not.

Decades later, David Fergusson concluded:

> [I]n broad outline it seems likely that the difficulties and disadvantages faced by contemporary Māori families are likely to represent the end of a long term historical process that has involved many components, including: the pressures faced by, and change in Māori culture and language following colonisation, the loss of land and economic power base experienced by Māori, increasing urbanisation of Māori and the general reduction of status and prestige (mana) of Māori people within the context of New Zealand society.

Fergusson does attach relative importance to each of these various phenomena. It is difficult to know how one might decide, for it is hard to test historical hypotheses. This study has given weight to urbanisation as the final stage in the process. It might be testable by looking at the difference in, say, incarceration rates of those living in rural and urban environments — although mobility between the two states may make it difficult to draw conclusions.

Ultimately these accounts of Māori over-representation in the criminal justice system — and, indeed, of over-representation in poor economic outcomes — involve a process of cumulative circular causation of one event influencing subsequent events, both for the individual and through generations.

From this perspective, the Department of Corrections report's policy recommendations are too narrow. Public interventions via the education, health and social support systems may be appropriate, but many will come too late to break a cycle of deprivation unless they target the family at an early stage.[95]

Bibliography

Department of Corrections (2007), *Over-representation of Māori in the Criminal Justice System: An Exploratory Report.* Department of Corrections, Wellington.

Duncan, L.S.W. (1971), 'Explanations for Polynesian Crime Rates in Auckland', *Recent Law,* October 1971.

Duncan, L.S.W. (1972), 'Racial Consideration in Polynesian Crime' in G. Vaughan (ed.) *Racial Issues in New Zealand: Problems and Insights.* Akarana Press, Auckland.

Fergusson, D.M. (2003), 'Ethnicity and Interpersonal Violence in A New Zealand Birth Cohort', in D.F. Hawkins (ed.) *Violent Crimes: Assessing Race and Ethnic Differences.* Cambridge University Press, Cambridge; New York.

CHAPTER 16 | **WEALTH AND HOUSING**

Wealth is a stock, whereas income is a flow. Some income comes from the return on wealth. Indeed, economists generalise this notion to say each person has 'human capital', or the capacity to work (in this context, it's classed as wealth), which generates their labour income. Human capital is high when someone is young, and depreciated as the individual nears death or retirement. Meanwhile, non-human wealth builds up for many in forms such as investments and passive income.

This means non-human wealth — the topic of this chapter — has a life cycle rising from low levels among the young to peak levels at retirement. As a consequence, it is much less equally distributed than income alone, or human plus non-human wealth. Because Māori are younger than non-Māori, they will be relatively more deficient in non-human wealth. However, this does not explain the entire difference.

Because people also have debt, non-human wealth is usually measured as 'net worth'. Debts are especially important where there is owner-occupier housing.

The Composition of Net Worth

Table 16.1 sets out the mean value of the assets and liabilities of Māori and Pākehā adults. The figures look low because they are average, including many without any assets at all.

An individual who says they are Māori-Pākehā appears in both columns.

Māori net worth averages just over a third of the Pākehā level. This is substantially less than their relative incomes, but part of the

Table 16.1: Individual Assets and Liabilities — Mean Value per Adult, 2015 ($000)

ASSET OR LIABILITY TYPE	MĀORI	PĀKEHĀ
Owner-occupier dwellings	$43,800	$113,300
Debt on owner-occupier dwellings	-$20,400	-$27,700
Net worth of owner-occupier dwellings	*$23,400*	*$85,600*
Other non-financial assets	$34,700	$80,600
Financial assets	$78,700	$205,500
Educational debt	-$3,100	-$2,400
Other individual liabilities	-$7,500	-$12,900
Individual net worth	**$126,200**	**$356,400**

Source: Statistics New Zealand (2016) *Household Net Worth Statistics*

difference is due to the different age profiles. Unfortunately, the data is not in a form in which we can say by how much.

That the age difference matters is evident in the educational debt. Among the actual holders of educational debt (which is not everyone included in Table 16.1), the Pākehā average is $20,000; the Māori average is $17,000, presumably reflecting the fact they take less expensive courses.

A further complication is that those who describe themselves as Māori-Pākehā are categorised in both columns. As a consequence, the gap between Māori-only and Pākehā-only is almost certainly larger than in the tabulation.

Together, Tables 14.2 and 14.3 suggest on average Māori investment incomes are about a fifth of Pākehā ones. This is somewhat less than what might be inferred from the relative levels of financial assets shown in Table 16.1 (the ratio is about two-fifths). That is probably mainly due to not including pension prospects in Table 16.1. If so, the inequality between Māori and Pākehā is even greater. (Additionally, Tables 14.1 and 14.2 exclude home ownership.)

It is also unfortunate there is no measure of the distribution of net wealth for each ethnicity. For what it is worth, the mean-to-median ratio is 7.6 for Māori and 3.0 for Pākehā, reflecting that a higher proportion of Māori have (near) zero assets.

Housing

A household's housing situation does not just affect its income; it greatly influences family wellbeing, health, education and other prospects.

Owner-occupier housing is the largest single asset in householders' portfolios, making up a third of the total measure (gross), or a quarter (net) of the debt on housing. (The figures for Māori are a third and a fifth, the latter reflecting relatively higher mortgages on houses occupied by Māori — probably because they are younger and have more recently purchased the housing.)

The value of the owner-occupied houses in Table 16.1 may seem low, but that is because they are spread across all members of the ethnic group. The mean value for a dwelling across owner-occupiers only is $187,00 for Māori and $259,000 for Pākehā. Even that is misleading, since the joint owners of a $300,000 house, say, would be recorded as $150,000 each. The net equity in the house after deducting the mortgage is $101,000 for Māori and $196,000 for Pākehā — almost double.

That applies only for owners. According to the 2013 Census, 56.7% of the adult Pākehā population owned or partly-owned their usual residence, in contrast to 28.2% of Māori. (These ratios are lower than home ownership because they are about people, not homes, and some adults live in homes that are owned without owning them themselves, e.g. adult children.) The import of these statistics coupled with those in the previous paragraph is that not only are Māori less likely to live in their own homes than Pākehā but their homes are also less valuable.

A Statistics New Zealand study found in the 1987–2004 period, including rental homes, some 13.8% of Māori households were overcrowded and required at least one additional bedroom — but only 3.7% of Pākehā households were as crowded. Overcrowding tended to fall for both households over the period. In 2004, Māori households were at 10% and Pākehā were just below 2.5% on this measure, compared with just over 15% and 5% respectively in 1987.

The series begins in 1987, too early to be able to identify the impact of the market liberalisation.

Conclusion

Not surprisingly, the available fragmentary evidence is that Māori have much lower net worth than Pākehā, not all of which can be explained by their being earlier in the life — and therefore wealth — cycle. One consequence is Māori experience inferior housing, with consequences for wellbeing, health and prospects.

This writer was unable to find any data supporting the notion that there was a convergence or divergence between Māori and Pākehā wealth distributions; there is very little data on the subject anyway.

Bibliography

Statistics New Zealand (2012), *Ethnicity and crowding: A detailed examination of crowding among ethnic groups in New Zealand 1986–2006*. Statistics NZ, Wellington.

Statistics New Zealand (2016), *Household Net Worth Statistics*. Statistics NZ, Wellington.

ENDNOTES

1. I am grateful to Piripi Walker for this translation.
2. Māori were not asked the same range of census questions, especially the economic ones, as non-Māori.
3. Urban in this context means in communities of 5,000 or larger; see chapter 1.
4. Until recently, the significant tertiary educational institutions for Maori were the army and to a lesser extent teachers colleges.
5. Oil production, in a parallel to the pre-1966 pastoral sector, has a resource rental that disappears when prices collapse.
6. The unemployed experience a dramatic reduction in their incomes, while unemployment weakens the rigidity of the linkages.
7. Other measures included fiscal and monetary policies aimed at maintaining full employment.
8. Such manufacturers were potentially competing against offshore production, which also employed low-skilled workers but at substantially lower wages.
9. A third option was that the wages of the unskilled would fall, attracting businesses to employ cheaper labour as a substitute for the skilled labour. However, that required the substitution to be technically feasible, while the required fall in the wage level was large; one estimate was by 17%.
10. Precise interpretation is complicated by new entrants to, and retirements from, the labour force, while some who registered more than once may not have been properly matched in the count. On the other hand, there were also workers made redundant who would have chosen not to register.
11. The exact amount is difficult to assess because of the limitations of the existing measures of wage rates: for instance, many do not allow for changes in labour force composition or payments above minimum set rates. There is no information on working conditions.
12. A further complication in assessing changes was that this was a period of 'disinflation'; the rate of inflation was falling from the double digits of the 1970s to low levels in the 1990s.

13. Relocation subsidies may have a role, although they do not work well for family workers.
14. Probably the most sophisticated form of this is the Danish 'flexicurity': flexibility in the labour market combined with supportive social security and an active labour market policy.
15. This is not a counsel of hindsight. For instance, Professor F.J.L. Young was advocating active labour market programmes in the mid-1960s.
16. Indeed, in 1938 the Treasury had recommended lower benefit rates for Māori because their incomes were lower. (McClure 1998).
17. Insofar as Rogernomics was replaced, the new regime was called 'Ruthanasia' after the new minister of finance, Ruth Richardson.
18. In 2016 an increase in child support of up to $25 a week for the first child was given.
19. The falling rate of inflation meant there was less tax revenue from fiscal drag.
20. Unions are also anathema to neoliberals.
21. That many beneficiaries could not work seemed to be almost irrelevant in these calculations, although sickness and invalids benefit levels were not cut as much as the unemployment benefit.
22. The income is market income less income tax plus social security benefits shared (equivalised) between members of a household (there is some allowance for economies of household scale).
23. See Table D6 of Perry (2017) for medians by ethnicity.
24. The proportions fell back following the mid-1990s improvement in the labour market and rising affluence for workers.
25. Different poverty lines would give similar conclusions.
26. A different poverty line from that used in the previous paragraph. However, we would expect the ratio to be much the same for different poverty lines.
27. However, other ethnic minorities, such as Pasifika, have similar rates in poverty.
28. As well as direct cuts to incomes, other measures increased the household spending on healthcare and education.
29. An additional distortion is that the ambulance drivers — medical personnel, teachers, those in the justice system — are much more politically vociferous in demanding resources to deal with the issues they address, while the fence builders — the parents — are not as effective at lobbying.
30. The problem is not unique. The housing sector faces the challenge of insufficient housing, plus the need to upgrade poor-quality housing built in the past.
31. The statute includes the Treaty in Māori, signed at Waitangi on 6 February 1840 and later. It also includes the version in English, signed only at Waikato Heads. This report refers to the document itself as Te

Tiriti to emphasise the Maori version has far greater standing. Many Maori see the issue as one not of text but of spirit.
32. Subsequent investigations have shown there is an enormous quantity of historical evidence — of varying quality, of course, but no worse than is normal. The Tribunal has usually been able to make unambiguous findings.
33. The term 'iwi' is used three times in the principles. In the latter two it roughly translates as 'tribes'. On the first occasion it may mean 'people'.
34. The Sealord deal, which was to settle Treaty claims in regard to ocean fishing rights, was also included in the envelope.
35. There may be non-financial parts of the settlements, such as involvement in the management of conservation resources.
37. Among the reasons for equity increasing more than profits is there were further proceeds from settlements.
38. The report covers trusts and companies that administer Māori freehold land, under Te Ture Whenua Māori Act 1993, the Māori Trustee, Māori trust boards, the Crown Forestry Rental Trust, Te Ohu Kaimoana, Aotearoa Fisheries Ltd, trusts and companies that receive and manage fisheries assets allocated under the Maori Fisheries Act 2004, and trusts and companies that receive and manage assets of the Treaty of Waitangi settlement redress process. Māori authorities are classified under section HF 2 of the Income Tax Act 2007.
39. Some 29% in Maori trusts, incorporations and other entities; 55% in assets of Maori employers; and 16% in assets of self-employed Maori.
40. Some marae have religious affiliations. Many educational institutions also have their own marae.
41. Gangs now also exist for Pasifika and Pākehā. Some are of mixed ethnicity.
42. Indicative of the pan-Māori nature of the Waipareira Trust, its 10-member board claimed 16 different iwi connections in 2015. No doubt the board's children have even more.
43. There is a peak organisation: the National Urban Māori Authority (NUMA).
44. While the scenario is for illustration rather than a likelihood, it is wise to remember at least one ex-Minister of Finance has advocated reducing government spending to 20% of GDP. (Douglas 1993)
45. While the changes would probably have little effect on iwi trust funds, we saw they contribute little directly to Māori household welfare. Iwi community providers would suffer in the same way as pan-tribal ones.
46. I am less sure that is what actually would happen; instead, many households would go without.
47. Ironically, because of their age structure Māori are not significant recipients of New Zealand superannuation, which has been indexed as the Royal Commission implicitly recommended.

48. At least, for the present, Māori-Pākehā. Other multiple ethnicities are likely to be too small in the sample for reliable analysis.
49. It is only possible to speculate because there is no data, but it may be that many (better-educated) Māori-Pākehā have a greater commitment to Māori culture (and even to te Reo) than the average sole-Māori.
50. In practice, one may learn of a Māori ancestor who had not been known previously.
51. Before 1981, the Census question was based on a 'hydraulic' (i.e. proportion of bloodlines) definition counting grand-parents or great-grandparents who were of only Māori descent.
52. It may well be that some respondents treat ethnicity and descent interchangeably; some of the public discussion does. Social scientists make a distinction. It is the reason this report uses 'Pākehā' rather than 'European'.
53. In 2013's Population Census, there were 4,212 people who said they were not of Māori descent, but that they were of Māori ethnicity. Presumably they include those without Māori ancestors who have married or been adopted into a Māori family and embrace its Māoriness.
54. Only those who were living in private occupied dwellings on the night of the 2013 Census.
55. According to the 2013 Population Census, about 3.5% of the entire population (including non-Māori) said they could speak Māori, again with a slight preponderance of females. The highest proportion was under the age of 15 years, but even here it was only 4.2%.
56. The projections expect Asians to exceed Māori in 2027, a conclusion particularly sensitive to assumptions about migration.
57. For a longer-term history, see chapter 2.
58. It is acknowledged here that there are other ethnicities in New Zealand — particularly Pasifika and Asian. However here, as elsewhere in the report, the focus is on Māori and Pākehā.
59. Unfortunately there is not a consistent locational series back to 1926 or 1951.
60. There are problems with other ethnic groups (e.g. the high proportion of Asians students who are visiting to study in New Zealand). Categorisation by gender is not readily available.
61. Qualification levels are scored as follows: bachelor degrees at 7.5 years, postgraduate and honours degrees at 8.5 years, doctorates at 12 years. Overseas secondary qualifications are treated as half level 3 certificate, half level 4. Those with two qualifications at the same level — say, two bachelor degrees — are treated as having only one. It is not possible to allow for differences of changes in the quality of qualifications.
62. If a separate country, Pākehā would be third in literacy, third equal in numeracy, and second in problem solving.
63. It is possible students who do well educationally are more likely to

give themselves multiple ethnicities: in which case those with poor educational achievement would be more likely to describe themselves as sole-Māori. This possibility is explored in the original reports, which note the 'both' gradients may minimise this effect, and are consistent with the hypothesis.
64. The term 'family' rather than 'whānau' is used, to emphasise the process is not peculiarly, nor inevitably, Māori.
65. In principle, someone who is working in a family business (or farm) may be classified as 'employed' as a 'relative assisting'.
66. Consider 100 young people, of whom 98 are in full-time education and training, 1 is in paid work and 1 unemployed. The apparent unemployment rate is 50%.
67. The data used here is census data. It depends on self-reporting.
68. If an adjustment for age composition is made it could be as high as 20%.
69. Comparable data from the 2001 Census is not available because of changing definitions.
70. The sharp fall in the mining sector probably reflects industry change, with low-skilled jobs becoming less important.
71. Although the 2013 Census has not published the required data, the Household Labour Force Survey drew the unsurprising conclusion that Māori are less likely to be employers or self-employed, together with the fact the gap seems to be diminishing.
72. At least up to about 1996, when the death registration form changed to a question that approximated the Census question.
73. The combination is for the existing population, not the (projected) mortalities for each cohort. This almost certainly underestimates the actual life expectancies, but the impact on differences is probably small.
74. The margins of errors for the estimates reported in this section are higher than usual.
75. These gains and losses are subject to margins of estimating error that may change the relativities.
76. This is income for only one year, not over a lifetime. That the income for a year seems to have a permanent effect reflects that the income in any year is co-related with life income.
77. There are bigger gains from shifting from low- to high-income status than from not smoking. (It is easier to stop smoking, though.) This is only reported for the entire population, but not ethnic groups. Carter et. al. (2010)
78. The sample is only of those who die, rather than the population as a whole.
79. Such as their higher incidence of smoking and their unwillingness to take action when there are early signs of cancer.
80. The median is the middle observation with equal numbers of observations (people) above and below.

81. The ethnic definitions are by 'prioritised ethnic group' before 2009 and by 'total response ethnic group' after 2007. Fortunately they are given for both in 2008 and are lapped to the second definition for the calculation. There is not a lot of difference.
82. Those aged 15–24 years are omitted because participation in tertiary education confuses the interpretation; as are those aged 65 and over, because retirement incomes also confuse the situation.
83. One might be tempted to compare the ratios shown in Table 6.2 with those in Table 6.1. Aside from the fact one is relative to Pākehā and the other to non-Māori, they reflect very different populations; one is earners, the other is all adults in the age group.
84. See note 82.
85. The averages for the period are shown. For both groups, the proportion of salary and wages was rising and the proportion from self-employment was falling. The government-transfers proportion was constant.
86. The 1981 results may be affected by the question being asked in a different way.
87. The division involves 'equivalence scales', which allow for the different needs of adults and children and for economies of scale.
88. The poverty measure is 60% of median CV (fixed line) AHC (after household costs).
89. The poverty measure is 60% of gross median income.
90. There is no data for other ethnic groups.
91. Initially the household survey was not held every year.
92. That this average is close to the 1990 figure adds to the credibility of the explanation for the lower rates in 1992 and 1994, which are years of very high unemployment.
93. The dependence is so heavy that had the chapter not cited the report, it might have been charged with plagiarism. This reflects both this writer's lack of expertise in the area, and an admiration for the quality of the report.
94. There are two longitudinal studies whose subjects have reached adulthood. Because their original samples were based in Christchurch and Dunedin, they involve smaller numbers of Māori than would a national sample. Given they still find the phenomenon reported here, as do international studies, one may conclude they demonstrate causal processes not exclusive to Māori, even if Māori are subject to a higher incidence of the characteristics that trigger them.
95. An indication of just how early is that drinking during pregnancy causes fetal alcohol spectrum disorders, which are associated with elevated criminality, among other things. Thus it is necessary to target young women who may get pregnant (since they may be drinking before they learn of their pregnancy). Moreover, they need to be in a supportive environment — so others also have to be involved. This convoluted example illustrates just how far back interventions may be necessary.

INDEX

Adult Skills Survey 84–85
Agriculture 16–20, 25, 27, 30, 32–39, 54, 95
Asians 69, 76, 84, 104
Auckland 18, 20, 23, 25–26, 59, 78–79
Australia 40, 42, 75, 79

Bay of Plenty 54, 78
Belshaw, Horace 19–21, 26–27, 30

Canterbury 28, 78
Charitable Trusts Act 59
Children 29, 48–49, 58–59, 75–77, 80, 89–90, 92–93, 96, 104, 108–110, 115–16
China 54
Christchurch 26, 59, 79
Closer Economic Relations 40
Crime 48, 58, 64–65, 112–18
Criminal justice system 64–65, 112–18

Demography 75–80
Department of Corrections 64, 112–13, 116–17
Disability Survey 100–101
Diseases 99–100
Domestic violence 48, 116
Durie, Judge Edward Taihakurei 51–52

Education 20–21, 27, 48, 63, 82–90
Employment 64, 91–97
Employment Contracts Act 41, 46–47
Europeans 11, 23, 27, 32, 36, 42, 69, 77, 100
European Union (EU) 36

Fertility 15, 24, 75, 77, 92
Fishing 17, 25, 27, 54, 95
Forestry 17, 25, 40, 54, 95

Gangs 58
GDP 54–55
Gender balance 76–77, 93, 99–102
Gisborne 18, 78–79
Great Depression 18, 23

Hamilton 26, 59, 79
Hāpai te Hauora 60
Health 48, 64, 98–103
Health Inequalities Research Programme (HIRP) 98, 103
Housing 24, 65, 102, 121–22

Incomes 41, 45–48, 64, 102, 104–111
Inflation 35–37, 39, 52, 110
Institute of Pacific Relations 19
Iwi corporates/Māori Authorities 50–56

Kukutai, Tahu 75

Manukau Urban Māori Authority 59
Māori broadcasting 60
Māori-Pākehā 67, 69, 86–89, 93, 119–20
Māori Welfare Act 59
Māori women in the labour force 29
Māori Women's Welfare League 58
Metge, Joan 25–26, 30
Migration 22–30, 36, 49, 58, 63, 65, 67, 76, 79, 116
More-market 38–44, 62, 65, 67
Mortality 15, 64, 76, 78, 98–101
MMP 45
Muldoon, Robert 36–39

Napier 18, 79
New Zealand Income Survey (NZIS) 104–107
New Zealand Wars 15, 19
Ngāi Tahu 71
Ngata, Sir Apirana 16, 19, 21, 27, 45, 71
Northland 78–79

OECD 34, 84–88

Pasifika 43, 69, 76, 84–85, 103–104, 109, 116
Peters, Winston 45
PISA (Programme for International Student Assessment) 85–87, 89
Pool, Ian 15, 19
Poverty 47–49, 108–109
Project Employment Programmes (PEP) 39

Ratana Church 45
Robinson, Peter 71
Rogernomics 38–41, 43
Royal Commission on Social Security 45–46, 66

Sealord 53
Sinclair, Keith 15
Smoking 101–102
Socioeconomic status (SES) 86–90
State Owned Enterprises Act 51
Statistics New Zealand 18, 53–54, 72–73, 77–80, 83, 92, 94–95, 120–21
Superannuation 80, 93
Survey of Family Income and Employment (SOFIE) 108
Sutherland, Ivor 19

Taupō 15
Tax 39, 41–42, 44, 46, 53, 59, 61, 104–108
Te Kōhanga Reo 48
Te Kupenga (Māori Social Survey) 72–74
Te Māngai Pāho (Māori Broadcast Funding Agency) 60
Te Puni Kōkiri (Ministry of Māori Development) 54–55, 60
Te Reo Māori 59–60, 63, 72–74
Te Rūnanga o Kirikiriroa Trust 59
Te Rūnanga o Ngā Maata Waka 59
Te Rūnanganui o Te Ūpoko o Te Ika 59
Te Whānau o Waipareira 57, 59
Treaty of Waitangi 50–53, 55

Urban Māori Authorities 59–61

Waikato 15, 53–54
Waikato Raupatu Lands Trust 53
Waitangi Tribunal 50–51, 58–59, 61
Wealth 65, 119–22
Wellington 18, 20, 26, 59, 78–79
Whānau Ora (Family Wellbeing) 60
Whanganui 18, 79
Wool 28, 32–40, 42
World War II 19, 23, 38, 42